# The Salvation Controversy

JAMES AKIN

# The Salvation Controversy

CATHOLIC ANSWERS
SAN DIEGO
2001

Published by Catholic Answers, Inc.
2020 Gillespie Way
El Cajon, CA 92020
(888) 291-8000 (orders)
(619) 387-0042 (fax)
www.catholic.com (web)
Cover design by Mary Lou Morreal
Printed in the United States of America
ISBN 1–888992–18–2

# Contents

# Preface

Good crystal gives off an unmistakable sound. If you strike it lightly with your forefinger, you'll hear the delicate *ping* that indicates: This is genuine; this is the real thing. But if the glass in your hand fails to make the telltale sound, you know that you're holding, at best, a glittering fake.

Something analogous happens in the world of the intellect. There are times when you just *know*, as if by instinct, and often before you're able to say exactly why, that an argument you're hearing is fatally flawed; it gives off something like the hollow *thunk* of cheap glass. But then there are those rare and precious times when you read a book or an article and—*ping!*—there's no mistaking: This is the real thing. At the banquet table of apologetics, James Akin's *The Salvation Controversy* is the finest of fine crystal.

Questions relating to salvation—especially faith vs. works, but also penance, purgatory, indulgences, and free cooperation with God's grace—have been neuralgic points in the dialogue between Catholics and Protestants. Serious people on every side have reasonably wondered whether dialogue can accomplish very much if anything, for what they have seen trumpeted as the fruit of ecumenical dialogue too often has involved falsification and betrayal of their respective traditions. This book should lay all such doubts to rest.

Mr. Akin knows and respects the Protestant tradition in which he was raised and the Catholicism he has come to embrace. He is not about to falsify either or to pretend that crucial differences do not exist. But he is also unwilling to allow theological slogans (like "faith alone") to distract us from significant points of agreement or allow verbal formulae (like "TULIP") to ease away the tense paradoxes of faith and freedom. His method is to follow Scripture and Tradition wherever they lead, and he is formidably equipped for the task with honesty, clarity of mind, and a super-abundance of logical rigor.

In apologetical circles, Mr. Akin was long ago nicknamed "The Terminator" precisely because of his logical skills and the remorse-less way he can wield them. Those skills are on frequent display in *The Salvation Controversy*. Though the sharp blade of dialectic is always tempered with charity, it still cuts straight and deep. So, readers, be warned: Some cherished theological nostrums may be reduced to a mass of tatters by the time Mr. Akin is finished with them.

Here I include myself among the bereaved. For many years I toyed with a certain interpretation of the meaning in Romans of "works." Then I read Mr. Akin's chapter on "Faith, Works, and Boasting." Few things in philosophy or theology deserve to be called definitive, but the argument of that chapter is surely a plau-sible candidate. At the very least it is a powerfully compelling case for one view of Pauline soteriology, and it demands a serious response from anyone who might hope to hold a different view.

That, in fact, could be said of this book as a whole. It is a serious work by a serious and supremely gifted apologist on a topic of central concern for everyone. If it elicits the response it deserves, then all of us, whatever our confessional commitments, will at least be clearer about what really does divide us. And what does not. Some notions, after all, deserve to be terminated.

— *Ronald K. Tacelli, S.J.*
Boston College

# Foreword

Shall I begin by confessing that I am not now, nor do I ever expect to become, a Scripture scholar? I am not even a convert, for heaven's sake. What I am, alas, is one of those countless cradle Catholics who grew up never reading the Bible, while serenely disdaining those who read little else. (Since joining a theology department where Scott Hahn holds forth, I have had, of course, to make certain adjustments.)

Under the circumstances, I am probably the least qualified to pass judgment on this book, except to say that its thesis, which Mr. Akin lays out with meticulous and unremitting precision, wholly inspires one to want to become ever more acquainted with God's word. That is finally the point, after all, of man's encounter with the sacred text: That we summon the wit sufficient to tease out the meaning God intended words to have, making possible, thereby, a living confrontation with God himself. "The intolerable wrestle with words and meanings," to recall T. S. Eliot's expressive image from *Four Quartets*. So I am very grateful to James Akin for such formidable resources of scholarship. Thanks to their adroit deployment, the cause of discipleship will likewise be strengthened and augmented.

And more. There is a line in Chesterton's *What's Wrong with the World* in which he reminds us that "the sincere controversialist is above all things a good listener." James Akin is a superb listener, and, having heard the arguments of Protestant Christianity (indeed, at one time they were his own), he is particularly situated to recognize and appreciate the peculiar rhythms and intonations of the language that Protestants use. It is a rare art and one which its greatest exemplar, St. Thomas Aquinas, exercised with singular dialectical skill. If one is to disarm one's adversary, said Thomas, one has got to know his arguments better even than he does.

9

It is, I believe, the best tribute I can pay to this book, that it manages so well to be both entirely sympathetic to the Protestant side and yet at the same time to leave it in ruins.

— *Regis Martin, S.T.D.*
Franciscan University
of Steubenville

# Introduction:
# On Words and Word-Fights

Over the last few centuries, a large number of books have been written on the subject of salvation. Most of them share these characteristics: (1) They focus exclusively on the subject of *eternal* salvation; (2) they focus in particular on the doctrine of justification; (3) they often ignore, in the interests of systematic theology, the way in which the Bible itself uses language; (4) they are written in a polemical, often hostile manner; and (5) due to the authors' not understanding the way other people express themselves, they mistakenly criticize views over which there is no disagreement in substance.

I want this book to be different. While it will discuss eternal salvation, I intend to show that the concept of salvation in the Bible is much broader than that. While this book discusses the doctrine of justification, this will not dominate the book to the detriment of other biblical themes relating to salvation. While this book addresses concerns of systematic theology, it focuses significantly on the way the Bible talks about salvation—the kind of *language* Scripture uses when addressing this subject. While this book takes a very definite position on many matters, it is not meant to be polemical or hostile toward those with other beliefs. Finally, while this book is critical of positions I believe to be in error, very great lengths are taken to understand the ways in which different groups of Christians express themselves on the subject of salvation.

I am convinced, having lived both as a Protestant and now as a Catholic, that the two sides often "talk past each other," each failing to take into account the different ways the other group uses words and phrases. It is my hope that I will be able to help various Catholics and Protestants "translate" the theological language of one group into the language of the other so that individuals on both sides can more adequately understand what their partners in dialogue (or controversy) actually *mean*, not just what they *say*.

From years of observing the theological scene, I am convinced that very often the two groups are led astray by terminology. They often perceive themselves to be in disagreement when actually they are not—or, at least, when the disagreement is not as sharp as the two groups believe it to be.

This is precisely the kind of situation that the apostle Paul attempted to prevent when he warned about quarreling over words. Paul orders Timothy to remind his flock of this "and charge them before the Lord to avoid disputing about words, which does no good, but only ruins the hearers" (2 Tim. 2:14).

Describing the person who is quarrelsome about words, Paul says he is "puffed up with conceit, he knows nothing; he has a morbid craving for controversy and for disputes about words, which produce envy, dissension, slander, base suspicions, and wrangling among men who are depraved in mind and bereft of the truth, imagining that godliness is a means of gain" (1 Tim. 6:4–5).

Contemporary Christians need to take Paul's words to heart. A great many individuals do not attempt to understand how their partners in dialogue or controversy use language, and when word-fights consequently erupt among them, the hearers can be ruined and the participants can have their own spiritual lives poisoned.

My hope is that this book will draw more people to a fuller understanding both of the richness of the way Scripture discusses the topic of salvation and of the ways other Christians discuss the topic.

—*James Akin*
Catholic Answers

# I

# Salvation Past, Present, and Future

## *"Have You Been Saved?"*

This is a question Protestants often pose when they are evangelizing, one that takes many people by surprise, including many Catholics. Some people are surprised because they never think about salvation, but Catholics tend to be surprised by it for a different reason: Catholics tend to focus on salvation as a future event, something that has yet to happen. As a result, the Protestant question "Have you been saved?" can sound presumptuous. But the question sounds very natural to Protestant ears because Evangelicals tend to conceive of salvation as a past event, something that happened to the believer at the very beginning of his life as a Christian.

Both of these conceptions of salvation are found in Scripture. For example, Paul speaks of salvation as a past event a number of times:

> [E]ven when we were dead through our trespasses, [God] made us alive together with Christ (by grace you *have been saved*) [Eph. 2:5].
>
> For by grace you *have been saved* through faith; and this is not your own doing, it is the gift of God [Eph. 2:8].

Since these passages speak of salvation as a past event, something that *has been done* to us, it is valid to conceive of salvation in this way. But this past aspect is only one dimension of salvation. There is an ongoing aspect to salvation as well, as is indicated in 1 Peter 1:8–9: "Without having seen him [Jesus] you love him; though

you do not now see him you believe in him and rejoice with un-
utterable and exalted joy. As the outcome of your faith you *obtain
the salvation of your souls.*" The Greek participle here translated as
"obtain" is in the present tense, which in Greek suggests ongoing
action.

The same idea of salvation as something that is taking place in
the present is found in the writings of St. Paul as well. For example, Philippians 2:12 says, "Therefore, my beloved, as you have
always obeyed, so now, not only as in my presence but much more
in my absence, *work out your own salvation* with fear and trembling"
(Phil. 2:12).

Salvation in the Bible is, therefore, also an ongoing process.
And it has a future aspect as well. There is a sense in which we
have not yet received salvation:

> Besides this you know what hour it is, how it is full time now for
> you to wake from sleep. For *salvation is nearer to us now* than when
> we first believed [Rom. 13:11].

> If any man's work is burned up, he will suffer loss, though he
> himself *will be saved*, but only as through fire [1 Cor. 3:15].

> [Y]ou are to deliver this man to Satan for the destruction of the
> flesh, that his spirit may *be saved in the day of the Lord Jesus* [1 Cor.
> 5:5].

These verses all speak of salvation as something that will happen
in the future. Therefore, salvation has past, present, and future
aspects.

A general summary of salvation, highlighting its past, present,
and future dimensions, would go something like this: "Salvation
is a process that begins when a person first becomes a Christian,
continues through the rest of his life, and is completed when he
stands before God in judgment." This summary allows the faithful Christian to do justice to all of the biblical data by saying, in
faith and hope, "I have been saved; I am being saved; and I will
be saved." It embraces all three of the dimensions of salvation that
are present in the biblical literature.

## *Other Aspects of Salvation*

In addition to salvation as a whole, Scripture also speaks of individual aspects of salvation called redemption, forgiveness, sanctification, and justification. These share the same past, present, and future dimensions that salvation as a whole does.

### REDEMPTION

First of all, redemption is sometimes spoken of as a present possession of believers, which suggests that they were redeemed sometime in the past.

> In him we *have redemption* through his blood, the forgiveness of our trespasses, according to the riches of his grace [Eph. 1:7].
>
> He has delivered us from the power of darkness and transferred us into the kingdom of his beloved Son, in whom we *have redemption*, the forgiveness of sins [Col. 1:13–14].

These verses indicate that redemption was given to the Christian at the beginning of his life with God, when he first entered Christ (*in* him and *in* whom we have redemption). But there is yet a future redemption awaiting us, for we also read in Scripture:

> And not only the creation, but we ourselves, who have the first fruits of the Spirit groan inwardly as we *wait for . . . the redemption* of our bodies [Rom. 8:23].
>
> [The Holy Spirit] is the first installment of our inheritance *toward redemption* as God's possession, to the praise of his glory [Eph. 1:14, NAB].
>
> And do not grieve the Holy Spirit of God, in whom you were sealed *for the day of redemption* [Eph. 4:30].

Therefore, redemption, like salvation in general, is something that occurs at different points in the Christian's life. There are no references in Scripture to redemption as a continuing process, but given the past and future dimensions of redemption, one may allow a sense in which we can be said to be in the process of "being redeemed" throughout the Christian life.

## FORGIVENESS

In numerous places, Scripture speaks of our forgiveness as something that has already occurred:

> In [Jesus Christ] we *have . . . the forgiveness of our trespasses*, according to the riches of his grace [Eph. 1:7].

> And be kind to one another, tenderhearted, forgiving one another, just as God in Christ also *forgave* you [Eph. 4:32].

> . . . in whom we *have . . . the forgiveness of sins* [Col. 1:14].

> . . . forbearing one another and, if one has a complaint against another, forgiving each other; as the Lord *has forgiven* you, so you also must forgive [Col. 3:13].

These passages show that forgiveness is something that has happened to us in the past, but the following passages are among those that speak of forgiveness as something that we must continue to appropriate. For example,

> And *forgive us our debts*, as we also have forgiven our debtors [Matt. 6:12].

> And the prayer of faith will save the sick man, and the Lord will raise him up; and if he has committed sins, he *will be forgiven* [Jas. 5:15].

> If we confess our sins, he is faithful and just, and *will forgive* our sins and cleanse us from all unrighteousness [1 John 1:9].

Therefore, forgiveness, like the other aspects of salvation, is both a past event and an ongoing process. And we know this process will not reach its fulfillment until we finally find mercy from the Lord on the last day, when our sins will be firmly, finally, and forever declared forgiven. Paul mentions this when he expresses his wish concerning Onesiphorus, that "the Lord grant him *to find mercy from the Lord on that Day*" (2 Tim. 1:18).

As a result, there is a sense in which forgiveness (God's mercy in this passage) is something that has yet to be realized.

## SANCTIFICATION

Evangelicals often place great emphasis on sanctification as a process Christians undergo. However, many in the Wesleyan tradition (Methodism, Holiness churches, the Church of the Nazarene, and some Pentecostal churches) tend to emphasize sanctification as an event that occurs at a definite point in the life of the believer. Both groups are correct in this. Sanctification is both a process and an event in our lives.[1] First, let us look at verses indicating sanctification as a past event in the Christian's life:

> But you were washed, you *were sanctified*, you were justified in the name of the Lord Jesus Christ and in the Spirit of our God [1 Cor. 6:11].

> [W]e *have been sanctified* through the offering of the body of Jesus Christ once for all [Heb. 10:10].

> How much worse punishment do you think will be deserved by the man who has spurned the Son of God, and profaned the blood of the covenant by which he *was sanctified*, and outraged the Spirit of grace? [Heb. 10:29].

These verses indicate the occurrence of sanctification as a past event in the life of the believer. But it is also an ongoing process, as the following verses indicate:

> [B]rethren, we beseech and exhort in the Lord Jesus, that as you learned from us how you ought to live and to please God, just as you are doing, you do so more and more. . . . For this is . . . *your sanctification*: that you abstain from immorality [1 Thess. 4:1, 3].

> Now may the God of peace himself *sanctify you completely*; and may your whole spirit, soul, and body be preserved blameless at the coming of our Lord Jesus Christ [1 Thess. 5:23].

---

[1] Unfortunately, Wesleyans place this event some time *after* initial justification, which is not correct.

> For both he who sanctifies and those who *are being sanctified* are all of one, for which reason he is not ashamed to call them brethren [Heb. 2:11, NKJV].

> For by one offering he has perfected forever those who *are being sanctified* [Heb. 10:14, NKJV].[2]

There is therefore abundant reason to say that sanctification is an ongoing process as well as a past event in the life of the believer. But what about sanctification as a future event in the life of the believer? It is harder to come up with verses illustrating this kind of sanctification, but that such sanctification exists may be easily deduced.

We know from various places in Scripture that we continue to stumble and sin all the way through this life, but we also know that we will not sin after the last day or after our death, whichever comes first. Therefore, we will be made holy in the sense that we no longer sin at all, and since sanctification means being made holy, when this event occurs we will be sanctified. There is thus a future event of sanctification in the life of the believer as well as a past and a present sanctification.

## JUSTIFICATION

In future sections, we will examine the nature of justification and how it relates to redemption, forgiveness, and sanctification, but here we should note that it, like the other aspects of salvation, has past, present, and future dimensions.

### Justification in the Bible

The following are some verses that show justification as a past event (emphasis added in each):

---

[2] In addition to these passages in Hebrews, see Rom. 12:2, 13:14; see also 2 Cor. 4:16 and Eph. 4:21–25.

Therefore, *having been justified* by faith, let us have peace with God. . . .[3] Through our Lord Jesus Christ, through whom also we have access by faith into this grace in which we stand [Rom. 5:1-2].

Since, therefore, we *are now justified* by his blood, much more shall we be saved by him from the wrath of God [Rom. 5:9].

But you were washed, you were sanctified, you *were justified* in the name of the Lord Jesus Christ and in the Spirit of our God [1 Cor. 6:11].

Justification is therefore clearly a past event in the life of the believer. Unfortunately, most Protestants have taken an inflexible position on verses implying this, concluding that justification is simply a once-for-all event, rather than also an ongoing, not-yet-completed process.

However attractive the single, once-for-all view of justification may be to some, serious biblical considerations weigh against it. This may be seen by looking at how the New Testament handles the story of Abraham. One of the classic Old Testament texts on justification is Genesis 15:6. This verse, which figures prominently in Paul's discussion of justification in Romans and Galatians, states that when God gave the promise to Abraham that his descendants would be as numerous as the stars of the sky (Gen. 15:5, cf. Rom. 4:18-22), Abraham "believed God and it was reckoned to him as righteousness" (Rom. 4:3).[4] This passage clearly teaches us that Abraham was justified at the time he believed the promise concerning the number of his descendants.

If justification is a once-for-all event rather than a process, that means that Abraham could not receive justification either *before* or *after* Genesis 15:6. However, Scripture indicates that he did both. First, the book of Hebrews tells us that "by faith Abraham obeyed

---

[3] In many Bibles this is given as an alternate translation, but the common version reading "we have peace" is based on inferior manuscripts.

[4] By definition, justification involves the bestowal of legal, actual, or behavioral righteousness.

when he was called to go out to a place which he was to receive as an inheritance; and he went out, not knowing where he was to go" (Heb. 11:8). Every Protestant will passionately agree that the subject of Hebrews 11 is saving faith. Indeed, Hebrews 11:1–2 tells us, "faith is the assurance of things hoped for, the conviction of things not seen. For by it the men of old received divine approval" (Heb. 11:1–2).

One does not get divine approval for one's faith unless it is saving faith. Thus the faith we are told in verse 8 that Abraham had must be saving faith. But *when* did he have this faith? The passage tells us: Abraham had it "*when he was called to go out to the place he would afterward receive as an inheritance.*" The problem for the once-for-all view of justification is that the call of Abraham to leave Haran is recorded in Genesis 12:1–4, three chapters before he is justified in 15:6. We therefore know that Abraham was justified well before (in fact, years before) he was justified in Genesis 15:6.

But if Abraham had saving faith back in Genesis 12, he was justified back in Genesis 12. Yet Paul clearly tells us that he was also justified in Genesis 15. So justification must be more than a once-for-all event. And just as Abraham received justification before Genesis 15:6, he also received it afterward, as we read in the book of James:

> Was not Abraham our father justified by works, when he offered his son Isaac upon the altar? You see that faith was active along with his works, and faith was completed by works, and the scripture was fulfilled which says, "Abraham believed God, and it was reckoned to him as righteousness"; and he was called the friend of God [Jas. 2:21–23].

In this instance, the faith Abraham had displayed in the initial promise of descendants was fulfilled in his actions (see also Heb. 11:17–19), thus bringing to fruition the statement of Genesis 15:6 that he believed God and it was reckoned to him as righteousness.

We see, therefore, that Abraham was justified on at least three different occasions: in Genesis 12, when he first left Haran and went to the promised land; in Genesis 15, when he believed the promise concerning his descendants; and in Genesis 22, when he offered his promised son on the altar. As a result, justification must be seen, not as a once-for-all event, but as a process that continues throughout the believer's life. In fact, the process even extends *beyond* the believer's life. This is shown by passages in Scripture where Paul indicates that there is a sense in which our justification is still future:

> For it is not the hearers of the law who are righteous before God, but the doers of the law who *will be justified* [Rom. 2:13].

> For no human being *will be justified* in his sight by works of the law, since through the law comes knowledge of sin [Rom. 3:20].

> For through the Spirit, by faith, we *wait for the hope of righteousness* [alternate translation, "we wait for the hope of justification"[5]] [Gal. 5:5].

Commenting on the second of these passages, the famous Protestant exegete James D. G. Dunn points out that Paul's statement alludes to Psalm 142:2. Dunn then remarks,

> The metaphor in the psalm is of a servant being called to account before his master, but in the context here [in Romans] the imagery of final judgment is to the fore. . . . Against the view that Paul sees "justification" simply as an act which marks the beginning of a believer's life, as a believer, here is a further example [in addition to 2:13] of the verb used for a final verdict, not excluding the idea of the final verdict at the end of life.[6]

Even apart from such verses, we could deduce a future justification on theological grounds alone. Protestants place much emphasis on the declarative aspect of justification (God's *declar-*

---

[5] The Greek word here is *dikaiosune*, which translates as "righteousness" or "justification." In either case, the text points to a future bestowal of righteousness and thus a future justification.

[6] *Word Biblical Commentary* (vol. 38a): *Romans 1–8* (Dallas: Word Books, 1988), 153.

*ing* one righteous), and they have placed special emphasis on the legal/courtroom contexts in which this declaration may occur. However, the ultimate courtroom declaration does not occur until the believer stands before God (at death and at the end of the world). So we may infer that the ultimate pronouncement of the believer as righteous does not take place in this life. We certainly are declared righteous (as well as made righteous) by God in this life, but the final, consummating declaration of our righteousness will not occur until the final judgment, therefore our final justification will not occur until that time. As a result, there remains a future justification for all believers.

### Justification in Protestant Teaching

As indicated, Protestants generally conceive of justification purely as a state rather than also as a process. However, a number of recent Protestant scholars, including James D. G. Dunn, E. P. Sanders, and Dale Moody, recognize that it is a process. What most Protestants do not know, even those who keep up with what contemporary Bible scholars are saying, is that some of the early Reformers also conceived of justification as a process in addition to being a state.

For example, the Swiss Reformer Martin Bucer regarded man as receiving a twofold justification. First he receives the *iustificatio impii* (justification of the impious), or primary justification, in which he is declared righteous before God, and then he receives the *iustificatio pii* (justification of the pious), or secondary justification, in which he is actually made to behave righteously.

Especially unknown to most non-Catholic Christians is that the very first Protestant of them all, Martin Luther, conceived of justification as a process. Luther scholar Paul Althaus explains:

> Luther uses the terms "to justify" . . . and "justification" . . . in more than one sense. From the beginning [of Luther's writings], justification most often means the judgment of God with which he declares man to be righteous. . . . In other places, however, the word stands for the entire event through which a man is essentially

made righteous (a usage which Luther also finds in Paul, Romans 5), that is, for both the imputation of righteousness to man as well as man's actually becoming righteous. Justification in this sense remains incomplete on earth and is first completed on the last day. Complete righteousness in this sense is an eschatological reality. This twofold use of the word cannot be correlated with Luther's early and later theology; he uses "justification" in both senses at the same time, sometimes shortly after each other in the same text.[7]

Luther himself wrote that "we understand that a man who is justified is not already righteous, but moving toward righteousness"[8] and that "our justification is not yet complete. . . . It is still under construction. It shall, however, be completed in the resurrection of the dead."[9]

We therefore see that, even though most Protestants deny that justification is both a process and a state, many contemporary Protestant scholars, like some of the early Protestant Reformers, recognize that justification is also a process.

---

[7] *The Theology of Martin Luther* (Philadelphia: Fortress, 1966), 226.

[8] *D. Martin Luthers Werke. Kritische Gesamtausabe* (Weimar, 1883), 39$^I$:83; *Luther's Works* 39$^I$:83 (Philadelphia and St. Louis, 1955), 34:152 (cited in Althaus, 237 n. 63).

[9] *Werke*, 39$^I$:252 (cited in op. cit.).

## 2

# Temporal and Eternal Salvation

### "Avoid Disputing about Words" (2 Timothy 2:14)

Too often the accusations Protestants and Catholics make against each other are based on misunderstandings; the two groups fail to appreciate that they are using terms differently. This is especially true when it comes to the doctrine of salvation. Over and over again, individuals get distracted by semantics while they agree on substance.

This is not to say there are not differences between Protestants and Catholics on matters of salvation. The common Protestant assertion that it is impossible for a true Christian to lose his salvation is a clear example. This is a serious difference—not merely a matter of terminology—and it must not be ignored, for it has dire spiritual consequences. There remain semantic differences, which must be identified, clarified, and removed from theological dispute.

### Two Kinds of Atonement

One of the greatest semantic misunderstandings concerns the way Catholics use the terms *salvation*, *atonement*, and *redemption*. Protestants have a distinctive and narrowly focused set of meanings for these terms, and when they read Catholic documents using these terms in larger senses, it appears to them that Catholics are denying the sufficiency of Christ's cross.

For example, it would upset many Protestants to read Catholic books and encounter the statement that one may atone for one's iniquity by faithfulness and love. "No one can atone for their sins," they might exclaim. "That is a denial of the sufficiency of the cross; only Christ can make atonement for us!"

Well, that's true. Only Christ can make atonement for us in one sense (the most important sense), because only he can deliver us from the eternal consequences of our sins. But this is not the only sense in which one can atone for sins. We can prove this because the statement that love and faithfulness atone for iniquity is straight out of the Bible. It happens to be from the book of Proverbs: "By love and faithfulness iniquity is atoned for, and by the fear of the LORD a man avoids evil" (Prov. 16:6).

Since it is true that only Christ can atone for our sins in the most important sense, we must conclude that Proverbs 16 is speaking of atonement in a *different* sense. Christ alone can atone for the eternal effects of our sins, so we must conclude that Proverbs 16 speaks of love and faithfulness resulting in a non-eternal atoning for sin; in other words, a temporal rather than an eternal atonement.

Unfortunately, most Protestants have lived so long with an incomplete presentation of the biblical doctrine of the atonement that they are aware only of the eternal aspect of atonement and find themselves at a loss when encountering passages in the Bible such as Proverbs 16:6.

Many Protestants have heard anti-Catholic preaching so often that they unconsciously are led to use a double standard when reading Catholic works. Reading the Bible, they accept its terminology concerning temporal atonement, but if Catholics in real life start using the same language the Bible uses on this subject, they are accused of teaching blasphemous, anti-Christian doctrines that deny the sufficiency of Christ's cross.

The only way to remedy this tendency is to point it out—to bring it into the light.

## Temporal and Eternal Salvation

In order to understand the idea of temporal atonement, we need to set it in its larger biblical context, which includes the concepts of temporal salvation and temporal redemption.

Most Christians quite naturally begin reading the Bible with the New Testament and only afterward go back to read the Old. This can cause perplexity about the use of certain terms, such as *salvation*, which are employed in different ways in the Old Testament.

The New Testament focuses primarily on the idea of eternal salvation—salvation from the eternal consequences of sin (hell) —but turning to the Old Testament, one finds the term *salvation* most often used to refer to salvation from temporal dangers such as war, famine, disease, oppression, and physical (rather than eternal) death. So great is the focus on temporal salvation that, of the over two hundred references to salvation in the Old Testament, it is very hard to find any that unambiguously refer to eternal salvation. A few examples will suffice to give a taste of the way the Old Testament most often speaks of salvation:

> I wait for thy salvation, O LORD. Raiders shall raid Gad, but he shall raid at their heels [Gen. 49:18–19].

> And Moses said to the people, "Fear not, stand firm, and see the salvation of the LORD, which he will work for you today; for the Egyptians whom you see today, you shall never see again. The LORD will fight for you, and you have only to be still" [Ex. 14:13–14].

> Because the LORD your God walks in the midst of your camp, to save you and to give up your enemies before you, therefore your camp must be holy, that he may not see anything indecent among you, and turn away from you [Deut. 23:14].

> Now therefore stand still, that I [Samuel] may plead with you before the LORD concerning all the saving deeds of the Lord which he performed for you and for your fathers [1 Sam. 12:7].

In these passages, the salvation the Lord gives concerns deliverance from dangers that the Israelites may or may not have brought on themselves by sin. It is simply a fact of life in this world that the wicked oppress the righteous and bring trouble on them, which is not always a punishment for sin (the fact that not all suffering is brought on by our sins is, of course, a major theme—in fact, the key point—of the book of Job). God saves from this kind of calamity, but he also saves from calamities that people bring upon themselves by sinning. For example, in Job we read:

> Man is also chastened with pain upon his bed, and with continual strife in his bones. . . . [But if] there be for him an angel, a mediator, one of the thousand, to declare to man what is right for him; and he is gracious to him, and says, "Deliver him from going down into the Pit, I have found a ransom" . . . then man prays to God, and he accepts him, he comes into his presence with joy. He recounts to men his salvation, and he sings before men, and says: "I sinned and perverted what was right, and it was not requited to me. He has redeemed my soul from going down into the Pit, and my life shall see the light" [Job 33:19, 23–24, 26–28].

In the above passage, the sickness is brought on the man by his own sin, so he is chastised, but an angel mediates for him and God saves him from the temporal calamities that had come upon him for his sins.

Of course, Job 33 is nowhere near the only Old Testament passage dealing with salvation from the temporal consequences of sin. This idea dominates the deliverance passages in the writings of the prophets, since the prophets are almost invariably talking about God's delivering his people from calamities they brought on themselves by their violence, oppression, and most of all their worship of false gods. The true God sent these punishments to chastise and correct them, and once the people repent, God then saves them from the distress their sins have caused.

What most people aren't aware of is that the idea of temporal salvation is also found in the New Testament. Though the New Testament focuses mostly on eternal salvation, the idea of temporal salvation is present as well. In fact, it is far more common than many would suppose. Let us look at just a few examples:

> And when he got into the boat, his disciples followed him. And behold, there arose a great storm on the sea, so that the boat was being swamped by the waves; but he was asleep. And they went and woke him, saying, "Save us, Lord; we are perishing!" [Matt. 8:23–25].
>
> And if those days had not been shortened, no human being would be saved; but for the sake of the elect those days will be shortened [Matt. 24:22].
>
> He saved others; he cannot save himself. He is the King of Israel; let him come down now from the cross, and we will believe in him [Matt. 27:42].
>
> Blessed be the Lord God of Israel, for he has visited and redeemed his people, and has raised up a horn of salvation for us in the house of his servant David, as he spoke by the mouth of his holy prophets from of old, that we should be saved from our enemies, and from the hand of all who hate us [Luke 1:68–71].

Another passage in Luke 1 that is a reference to temporal salvation is nearly always misread as a reference to eternal salvation. It occurs in the Magnificat:

> And Mary said, "My soul magnifies the Lord, and my spirit rejoices in God my Savior, for he has regarded the low estate of his handmaiden—for behold, henceforth all generations will call me blessed; for he who is mighty has done great things for me, and holy is his name. And his mercy is on those who fear him from generation to generation. He has shown strength with his arm, he has scattered the proud in the imagination of their hearts, he has put down the mighty from their thrones, and exalted those of low degree; he has filled the hungry with good things, and the rich he has sent empty away. He has helped his servant Israel, in remembrance of his mercy, as he spoke to our fathers, to Abraham and to his posterity for ever" [Luke 1:46–55].

This passage is often used by Protestants in an attempt to show that Mary was a sinner because she refers to God as her Savior.

This is an unnecessary effort, since Catholic theology *agrees* that God was Mary's Savior. In fact, he saved her in a more spectacular way than he had saved others—not only from the consequences of having fallen into sin but even from falling into sin in the first place—making her, as the *Catechism of the Catholic Church* puts it, "the most excellent fruit of redemption" (CCC 508). Mary is the most *saved* person there is, since by God's grace she was saved from things he let the rest of us fall into.

Not only is it fruitless to argue that Mary must be a sinner because she has a Savior, it is also a misreading of this passage, stemming from the false assumption that all New Testament references to salvation are references to eternal salvation. Whenever one encounters a reference to salvation in the Bible, one must ask whether temporal or eternal salvation is under discussion. Thus we must ask ourselves how Mary is conceiving of God's salvation in this passage—as temporal or eternal?

When we do this, it seems that the idea of God as Savior from temporal circumstances is at the forefront of her mind. "My spirit rejoices in God my Savior," she declares, "*for* he has regarded the low estate of his handmaiden—for behold, henceforth all generations will call me blessed; for he who is mighty has done great things for me." As the explanatory connective *for*[1] indicates, the reason Mary rejoices in God as her Savior is that "he has regarded the low estate of his handmaiden" and done marvelous things for her. God has thus saved her from her low estate and given her an exalted estate so that she will be remembered and honored forever: "for behold, henceforth all generations will call me blessed."

That salvation from her lowly temporal circumstances is what Mary has in mind is reinforced as she then proceeds to name several kinds of temporal salvation ("He has shown strength with his arm, he has scattered the proud in the imagination of their hearts, he has put down the mighty from their thrones, and exalted those of low degree; he has filled the hungry with good things, and the rich he has sent empty away. He has helped his servant Israel, in

---

[1] Greek, *hoti*, which translates as "because," "since," "that," "for."

remembrance of his mercy, as he spoke to our fathers, to Abraham and to his posterity for ever") and by the parallel canticle in which Zechariah proclaims the praise of God as temporal Savior (Luke 1:68–75).

Fortunately, some Protestants, including even the quite anti-Catholic R. C. Sproul, are open to the fact that Mary's reference to God as Savior refers to his role as temporal Savior. Their admission of this fact will lead, one hopes, to a broader understanding among Protestants of the biblical teaching on temporal salvation.

As with the Old Testament, the New Testament includes the idea of salvation from the temporal consequences of sin. We find a rather comical example of this in Matthew's account of the apostles' seeing Jesus walking toward them on the Sea of Galilee:

> And Peter answered him, "Lord, if it is you, bid me come to you on the water." He said, "Come." So Peter got out of the boat and walked on the water and came to Jesus; but when he saw the wind, he was afraid, and beginning to sink he cried out, "Lord, save me." Jesus immediately reached out his hand and caught him, saying to him, "O man of little faith, why did you doubt?" [Matt. 14:28–31].

Here the temporal consequence from which Peter is saved is drowning. A point of special interest in this text is the way Jesus saves him—simply by reaching out a hand and pulling him up. To save Peter, Jesus did something that any one of us could have done if we had been close enough to Peter and had a firm base to stand upon. Jesus, of course, was standing on the water, but anyone standing on a boat, a rock, or a platform could have done the same thing.

## Temporal and Eternal Saviors

The passage where Jesus saves Peter from drowning reveals to us a very important point about the mechanics of temporal salvation: One does not have to be God to be a temporal savior, which is something to which I can testify from very recent experience. The day before I began this chapter, I went to a doctor to see about getting some relief for lower back pain I had been experiencing. Contrary to all advice, contrary to my own knowledge of what I should have done, I had lifted some heavy objects, bending at the waist rather than the knees. I have been suffering the consequences. The doctor prescribed an anti-inflammatory for my back pain and thus helped save me from the consequences of my mistake. And, under the providence of God, I am sure that it was the Lord's will that I receive this temporal salvation.

This situation of God's using a physician to heal someone who has done wrong is reflected in sacred Scripture. The best passage for showing this is one that the Protestant Reformers, unfortunately, cut out of the Bible, but the principles it expresses are so good that most Protestants would wish it were in their Bibles for its value in combating "health-and-wealth" preachers. The passage is from the book of Sirach:

> Honor the physician with the honor due him, according to your need of him, for the Lord created him; for healing comes from the Most High, and he will receive a gift from the king. . . . The Lord created medicines from the earth, and a sensible man will not despise them. . . . [T]he pharmacist makes . . . a compound. His works will never be finished; and from him health is upon the face of the earth. My son, when you are sick do not be negligent, but pray to the Lord, and he will heal you. . . . And give the physician his place, for the Lord created him; let him not leave you, for there is need of him. There is a time when success lies in the hands of physicians, for they too will pray to the Lord that he should grant them success in diagnosis and in healing, for the sake of preserving life. He who sins before his Maker, may he fall into the care of a physician [Sir. 38:1–2, 4, 8–9, 12–15].

There can be no disputing that God sends some people to be temporal saviors, for even the Scriptures acknowledged by Protestants flatly describe individuals in this manner:

> And the anger of the LORD was kindled against Israel, and he gave them continually into the hand of Hazael king of Syria and into the

hand of Ben-hadad the son of Hazael. Then Jehoahaz besought the
LORD, and the LORD hearkened to him; for he saw the oppression of
Israel, how the king of Syria oppressed them. Therefore the LORD
*gave Israel a savior,* so that they escaped from the hand of the Syrians;
and the people of Israel dwelt in their homes as formerly [2 Kgs.
13:3‒5].

Nevertheless they were disobedient and rebelled against thee and
cast thy law behind their back and killed thy prophets, who had
warned them in order to turn them back to thee, and they committed great blasphemies. Therefore thou didst give them into the
hand of their enemies, who made them suffer; and in the time of
their suffering they cried to thee and thou didst hear them from
heaven; and according to thy great mercies *thou didst give them saviors
who saved them* from the hand of their enemies [Neh. 9:26‒27].

The exiles in Halah who are of the people of Israel shall possess
Phoenicia as far as Zarephath; and the exiles of Jerusalem who are
in Sepharad shall possess the cities of the Negeb. *Saviors shall go up
to Mount Zion* to rule Mount Esau; and the kingdom shall be the
LORD's [Obad. 20‒21].

In each of these cases, God sends temporal saviors to deliver his
people from the temporal consequences of their sins. We therefore have to say that God is the only eternal Savior but that God
uses numerous people as temporal saviors.

## Forgiveness and Fellowship

With background in the concepts of temporal versus eternal salvation and temporal versus eternal saviors, we can proceed further
in understanding the related biblical teachings.

We opened with the statement from Proverbs 16:6 that love and
faithfulness atone for iniquity and noted that the verse referred
to temporal atonement. Now that we have become more familiar
(and, one hopes, more comfortable) with the Bible's teaching on
the subject, we are ready to delve into the meaning of Proverbs
16:6 a little more deeply.

The term that this verse uses for "atone" is *kapar* and the word for "atonement" is *kippur*. Unfortunately, the nature of the biblical concept of atonement is not well understood. One reason for this is that there is an Arabic word related to *kapar* that means "cover," and this has distracted some theologians. Many therefore suggest that the idea of atonement is that of covering over sin, hiding or concealing it from God's sight. This plays well with the common Protestant idea that we are only made legally righteous in justification, that God covers over our sins and does not look at them. But this understanding of atonement doesn't work. As Protestant scholar R. Laird Harris explains: "There is, however, very little evidence for this view. The connection of the Arabic word is weak, and the Hebrew root is not used to mean 'cover.' "[2]

By an examination of the Hebrew words related to *kapar*, however, one can get a better insight into its meaning. *Kapar* does not concern covering over; rather, it suggests the idea of providing compensation, making the concept similar to the idea of redemption or "buying back" that which was lost. Harris explains that *kapar* means

> "to atone by offering a substitute." The great majority of the usages concern the priestly ritual of sprinkling of the sacrificial blood and thus "making an atonement" for the worshipper. There are forty-nine instances of this usage in Leviticus alone, and no other meaning is there witnessed. The verb is always used in connection with the removal of sin or defilement, except for Gen. 32:20, Prov. 16:14, and Is. 28:18, where the related meaning of "appease by a gift" may be observed. It seems clear that this word aptly illustrates the theology of reconciliation in the [Old Testament]. The life of the sacrificial animal specifically symbolized by its blood was required in exchange for the life of the worshipper.[3]

Atonement brings about salvation. The eternal atonement of Christ brought about eternal salvation for us, and temporal atone-

---

[2] R. L. Harris, G. L. Archer, B. K. Waltke, *Theological Wordbook of the Old Testament*, (Chicago: Moody Press, 1980), 1:452–453.

[3] Ibid., 453.

ment brings about temporal salvation, or freedom from the temporal consequences of sin.

In this case, the consequence of iniquity that love and faithfulness repair is the constriction placed on one's relationship with God even if the eternal effects of the sin are forgiven. Protestants, especially those who assert that it is impossible to lose salvation, often stress the difference between forgiveness and fellowship. They point out, rightly, that even when the eternal consequences of one's sins have been forgiven, one's relationship with God can still be impaired. Thus, even though one is in a state of eternal forgiveness—what Catholics call the state of grace—one may still need to repent in order to be restored to fellowship, or at least full fellowship, with God.

Such impairment of one's fellowship with God is, of course, a temporal rather than an eternal consequence of sin, and by repenting—by being faithful and loving under the impetus of God's grace—the relationship one has with God will grow in strength and thus one's level of fellowship with God will grow. It is in this sense that love and faithfulness atone for iniquity. The love and faithfulness that the repentant sinner now shows serve to illustrate his desire to make up for his former lack of love and faithfulness.

# 3

# Two Other Kinds of Salvation

The previous chapter spoke of what might be called temporal and eternal salvation and their relationships to various doctrines. However, the Scriptures also speak about salvation in other ways. This chapter considers two particular ways Scripture speaks about salvation, which for the sake of convenience we will call "middle salvation" and "general salvation."

## *Middle Salvation*

Middle salvation is what happens when God uses one person as an agent to bring eternal salvation to someone else. By preaching the gospel, rebuking sinners, administering the sacraments, etc., one human may, under the providence of God, save another human being (bring him eternal salvation). This language rubs many Protestants the wrong way, but it is the language of the New Testament:

> Now I [Paul] am speaking to you Gentiles. Inasmuch then as I am an apostle to the Gentiles, I magnify my ministry in order *to . . . save* some of [my fellow Jews] [Rom. 11:13–14].

> Wife, how do you know whether you *will save* your husband? Husband, how do you know whether you *will save* your wife? [1 Cor. 7:16].

> To the weak I [Paul] became weak, that I might win the weak. I have become all things to all men, that I might by all means *save* some [1 Cor. 9:22].

Take heed to yourself and to your teaching; hold to that, for by so doing you will *save* both yourself and your hearers [1 Tim. 4:16].

My brethren, if any one among you wanders from the truth and some one brings him back, let him know that whoever brings back a sinner from the error of his way *will save* his soul from death and will cover a multitude of sins [Jas. 5:19-20].

And convince some, who doubt; *save* some, by snatching them out of the fire; on some have mercy with fear, hating even the garment spotted by the flesh [Jude 22-23].

As the above verses show, the Bible speaks of humans saving other humans, not just with respect to temporal salvation (from physical disasters, illnesses, wars, etc.), but with respect to eternal salvation as well. Of course this does not mean that humans bestow eternal salvation on other humans the way Christ does, by earning it for them, but it does mean that humans serve as agents of Christ in bringing his graces to others (a point Martin Luther makes very well in the section on baptism in his *Long Catechism*).

Yet for many Protestants this language is embarrassing, and any talk of one mortal human saving another makes them extremely uncomfortable. Catholics have no problem with this concept, however, because they have not rejected this form of biblical language.

It should be noted that Scripture speaks of individuals saving themselves (e.g., 1 Tim. 4:16, above). Since we cannot earn eternal salvation ourselves, and since mere temporal salvation does not seem in view in these passages, this language is best understood in terms of the "middle salvation" category. The middle salvation mode of speech thus includes not only references to one individual helping to bring eternal salvation to another but also references to one's own pursuit of eternal salvation.

## General Salvation

One final mode of speaking about salvation needs to be noted. We will call this the "general salvation" mode of speech. In the general mode, the term *salvation* is used without differentiation between temporal, middle, and eternal deliverance.

It would be a mistake to assume, merely because there are three kinds of saving spoken of in Scripture, that every use of the term *salvation* must always refer specifically to one of them. This would be as great a mistake as assuming—because there are two kinds of humans—male and female—that every use of the term *human* must either have in mind exclusively males or exclusively females. Just as the term *human* can refer to both male and female without differentiation, *salvation* can refer to temporal, middle, and eternal salvation without specifying any particular one of them.

This general way of speaking about salvation is found in some descriptions of God as Savior. In many passages, like the ones previously discussed, one particular aspect of his role as Savior may be in the forefront. He may in a given passage be spoken of as a Savior from temporal distress or as a Savior from eternal agony, or he may be spoken of as a Savior in a general sense without specifying either kind of salvation he gives.

This concept of general salvation underlies passages of Scripture that speak of humans participating in the sufferings and work of Christ:

For as we share abundantly in Christ's sufferings, so through Christ we share abundantly in comfort too [2 Cor. 1:5].

Now I [Paul] rejoice in my sufferings for your sake, and in my flesh I complete what is lacking in Christ's afflictions for the sake of his body, that is, the church [Col. 1:24].

But rejoice in so far as you share Christ's sufferings, that you may also rejoice and be glad when his glory is revealed [1 Pet. 4:13].

This idea of uniting our sufferings with Christ's and sharing in his sufferings is something Catholics talk about all the time, but Protestants almost never do. This is because they have almost totally lost the language of general salvation, which makes the above quotations intelligible.

Humans do share in Christ's sufferings in the sense that they are persecuted for the sake of Christ or because they suffer in the service of Christ, and both of these forms of suffering bring salvation to others. Being persecuted for Christ brings salvation to others, for "the blood of the martyrs is the seed of the Church" (Tertullian, *The Apology* 50), and by suffering in the service of Christ, one spreads the gospel and brings salvation to others.

In all these cases, ordinary humans merely serve as temporal or middle saviors, not eternal saviors as Christ is. Humans may bring temporal salvation to others by direct action (such as pulling them out of a flood) or by indirect action (such as praying for those in a flooded area). And they may bring Christ's eternal salvation to others by direct action (such as preaching the gospel or administering the sacraments) or by indirect action (such as praying for conversions). But in no case do humans earn eternal salvation for others and thus serve as eternal saviors the way Christ does.

Catholics are comfortable with the "general salvation" mode of speech, which is the one Paul is using when he says he completes "what is lacking in Christ's afflictions." Paul's understanding is still maintained by Catholics today—that with regard to eternal salvation, Christ's afflictions not only lacked nothing, but their value was infinite and thus fully adequate to secure the salvation of the world.

Paul's statement that he makes up what is lacking in Christ's sufferings—if said by anyone but Paul—would be horrifying to Protestant ears. If a typical Evangelical Protestant heard a Catholic make such a statement, not knowing or remembering that Paul had said exactly the same thing in Scripture, he might denounce the Catholic as a heretic. He would be led to make this denunciation by a legitimate desire to preserve the uniqueness of Christ as Savior coupled with a lack of familiarity with the Bible's manner of speaking of salvation in a general way, that is, without differentiating the role an ordinary human is playing with respect to temporal, middle, or eternal salvation.

This is the reason Protestants are disturbed when they hear Catholics talking about Mary and the saints as playing a role in our salvation by their prayers. They fail to recognize that the language of general salvation is being used and that, as in the Bible, ordinary humans are being spoken of in a manner that does attribute to them a role in salvation but not the role of serving as eternal saviors, which is something only Christ can do. Mary and the saints do, like living humans, serve as temporal and middle saviors, though in their case they do this through indirect action only (that is, through prayers) since they are not on earth and cannot take direct action (such as pulling someone out of a flood, preaching the gospel, etc.).

Protestants commonly fail to recognize the language of general salvation when they read Catholic writings about the sacraments. For example, professional anti-Catholic Dave Hunt has in the past few years been making much of the fact that the first page of the Constitution on the Sacred Liturgy (the first document of Vatican II) says that "it is the liturgy through which, especially in the divine sacrifice of the Eucharist, the work of our redemption is accomplished" (*Sacrosanctum Concilium* 2). Hunt proceeds on a misunderstanding and makes incorrect, animated declarations to the effect: "You see! The liturgy saves us! Vatican II preaches a false gospel from the very first page!"

Yet Hunt errs by failing to recognize the language of general salvation. A Catholic would not say the liturgy provides salvation in the same mode that Christ's death on the cross provides salvation. Christ died once for all, and that is a completed act. When the liturgy is celebrated, it does not provide any new redemption that was not made by Christ's death on the cross. It does not add to the merits of Christ's death. The Church, as at the Council of Trent, has been very explicit that the liturgy and the Eucharist in no way substitute for or supplement what Christ did on the cross —that sacrifice being more than sufficient for all our needs.

Instead, it is through the liturgy and the Eucharist that what Christ did on the cross is *applied* to us—playing a role with respect to "middle salvation" (either by applying to us eternal graces or by elevating our thoughts and reinforcing habit-patterns such that we will adhere to God more tightly and pursue Christ more zealously). Hunt has failed to see this because he, like many Protestants, has lost the ability to recognize the language of general salvation.

The same is also true when Protestants hear Catholics talk about indulgences and their basis on the merits of Christ and the saints. Oddly, Protestants seem to have developed their own language about this doctrine which they *believe* Catholics use, though in reality Catholics don't. For example, Protestants will often say Catholics believe in something called "the transfer of merit," but Catholics never use that term. I have checked many Catholic reference works and have never found it. I have also checked with many scholars, Catholic all their lives, who consistently deny ever having heard of "the transfer of merit." That is a Protestant phrase, not a Catholic one. Catholics never speak of God *transferring* merit from one person to another. The 1910 *Catholic Encyclopedia* puts it this way:

> Each good action of the just man possesses a double value: that of merit and that of satisfaction, or expiation. Merit is personal, and therefore it cannot be transferred; but satisfaction can be applied to others, as St. Paul writes to the Colossians (1:24) of his own works: "Who now rejoice in my sufferings for you, and fill up those things which are wanting of the sufferings of Christ, in my flesh, for his body, which is the Church" [*Catholic Encyclopedia*, 7:784].

In the same way, Protestants also talk about the treasury of merits consisting of Christ's merits and the "surplus merits" of the saints, which are said to be "more than what was needed for their salvation"—as if there were some magical, unspecified amount of merit that one needs to accumulate in order to go to heaven, an amount which some people but not others exceed. Needless to say, there is nothing like this in the official documents; nor do

Catholic theologians talk this way. It's a fundamental misunderstanding of Catholic thought. As a matter of fact, the major historic document discussing the basis for this doctrine, *Unigenitus*, a bull written in 1343 by Pope Clement VI, expressly states that "to the mass of this treasure [of the infinite merits of Christ] the merits of the Blessed Mother of God and of *all the elect from the first just one to the last*, are known to give their help."

A Catholic using language to the effect of doing more than what is required for his salvation would not be referring to his *eternal* salvation, since Christ did all that was needed, and the minute one is justified, one is given eternal life. He would be referring, rather, to temporal salvation, or removal of the temporal barriers (divine discipline, penance, purification/sanctification in purgatory) between himself and final entrance into glory. He would thus be using a kind of "middle salvation" language.

One can see the confusion that has been caused because Protestants generally have lost the ability to distinguish between the language of eternal, temporal, middle, and general salvation. It is truly tragic that those who pride themselves the most on fidelity to the Bible have ended up losing the ability to identify these modes of speech in the language in the Bible itself.

# 4

# Doing Penance

In the chapter on temporal and eternal salvation, we commented on the statement from Proverbs 16:6 that "by loyalty and faithfulness iniquity is atoned for, and by the fear of the LORD a man avoids evil," and we noted that this verse refers to temporal atonement. Now we are ready to look at the concept of temporal atonement in more depth, for the biblically mandated practice of temporal atonement is the same as the practice of doing penance for one's sins. Acts of penance can be formal, such as setting a day of fasting, or informal, such as deliberately going out of one's way to be nice to someone.

In this regard, it is helpful to note that Protestants, especially those who assert that it is impossible to lose salvation, often stress the difference between forgiveness and fellowship. They will point out, rightly, that even when the eternal consequences of one's sins have been remitted, one's relationship with God can still be impaired. Thus even though one is in a state of forgiveness—the state of grace—one may still need to repent in order to be restored to fellowship, or at least full fellowship, with God.

In this sense, love and faithfulness atone for iniquity, which is the concept behind the historic Christian practice of penance. Anti-Catholics often attack the practice of doing penance to atone, or make reparations, for one's sins. They fail to realize, however, that the atonement that penance involves is temporal rather than eternal. Catholics are not trying to pay off the eternal debt of their sins by doing penance. Christ paid all that off in one fell swoop almost two thousand years ago. No more payment of the eternal debt of our sins is needed. No more payment of the eternal debt of our sins is possible. And though it would surprise many Protestants to learn it, this precise point was vigorously and vociferously stressed by the medieval Catholics that Protestants (inaccurately) credit with coming up with the whole system of penance.

This fact is often ignored and sometimes even denied in Protestant preaching, as when some, especially Calvinists, claim that Christ's sufferings were sufficient but *only* sufficient (i.e., not *more than* sufficient) to cover the sins of the elect; but the medieval Christians understood this point very well.

For example, the great medieval saint and doctor of the Church, Thomas Aquinas, writes in the *Summa Theologiae* (hereafter ST) that

> by suffering out of love and obedience, Christ gave more to God than was required to compensate for the offense of the whole human race. First of all, because of the exceeding charity [on account of] which he suffered; secondly, on account of the dignity of his life which he laid down in atonement, for it was the life of one who was God and man; thirdly, on account of the extent of the Passion, and the greatness of the grief endured, as stated above. And therefore Christ's Passion was not only a sufficient but a superabundant atonement for the sins of the human race; according to 1 John 2:2: "He is the propitiation for our sins: and not for ours only, but also for those of the whole world" [ST III:48:2].

By no means unique to Aquinas, this has been the common teaching of Catholics both before and since he wrote, as it is to this day. As the *Catechism of the Catholic Church* states, "The Christian tradition sees in this passage [Gen. 3:15] an announcement of the 'New Adam' who, because he 'became obedient unto death, even death on a cross,' makes amends superabundantly for the disobedience of Adam" (CCC 411). Yet this teaching puzzles Protestants who deny the need for acts of penance. "If Christ's sufferings were more than sufficient," they ask, "why then should we do penance?"

This question has three answers. First, regarding the distinction between forgiveness and fellowship, we saw that even those who are in a state of forgiveness may have impaired fellowship with God and need to correct this. Acts of sorrow over one's sins (penance) are a key way this is done. Thus, as we will see below, people in both testaments of the Bible would do penance in order to restore fellowship with God by mourning for their sins.

Second, when God remits the eternal penalty for a sin, he may (and often does) choose to leave a temporal penalty to be dealt with. When he forgave David for his sin concerning Uriah, he still left David the temporal punishment of having his infant son die and having the sword pass through his house (2 Sam. 12:13ff.). Similarly, when Moses struck the rock a second time, God forgave him (for Moses was obviously one of the saved, as his appearance on the Mount of Transfiguration illustrates), though he still suffered the temporal penalty of not being allowed to go into the promised land (Num. 20:12).

Why does God leave some temporal penalties in place when he removes the eternal penalties for our sins? Part of this is a mystery, since Christ's sufferings are sufficient to cover even the temporal penalties of our sins. However, one reason is to teach us our lesson. We often learn our lesson far better if we have not just head knowledge that what we did was wrong, but experiential knowledge of its wrongness through feeling negative consequences. Thus parents may allow their children to experience the consequences of their folly or may tell them, "Look, I love you and I've forgiven you, but you're still going to be grounded." Similarly, in the Bible we read:

And have you forgotten the exhortation which addresses you as sons?—"My son, do not regard lightly the discipline of the Lord, nor lose courage when you are punished by him. For the Lord disciplines him whom he loves, and chastises every son whom he receives." It is for discipline that you have to endure. God is treating you as sons; for what son is there whom his father does not discipline? If you are left without discipline, in which all have participated, then you are illegitimate children and not sons. Besides this, we have had earthly fathers to discipline us and we respected them. Shall we not much more be subject to the Father of spirits and live? For they disciplined us for a short time at their pleasure, but he disciplines us for our good, that we may share his holiness. For the moment all discipline seems painful rather than pleasant; later it yields the peaceful fruit of righteousness to those who have been trained by it. Therefore lift your drooping hands and strengthen your weak knees, and make straight paths for your feet, so that what is lame may not be put out of joint but rather be healed [Heb. 12:5-13].

We see, thus, that God often leaves in place a portion of the temporal retribution we deserve, and that this chastisement, on the model of punishing a child, may have a rehabilitative effect on us. Penance is one way in which we willingly embrace this discipline in order to learn from it, just as a godly child may consciously embrace his parent's discipline (see the chapter on indulgences for further discussion of this issue).

Third, humans have an inner need to mourn over tragedies, just as Christ himself mourned over tragedies, as when he wept at the tomb of Lazarus (John 11:35). This inner need must not be short-circuited; humans must be allowed to feel grief over tragedies. And, because our sins are tragedies, we have a natural need to mourn over them. We also have an inner need to make a gesture of reparation for our sins when real reparation is impossible. Penance allows us to feel the grief we naturally have and need to express this grief when we have done wrong and repented.

Unfortunately, in Evangelical circles this process is often short-circuited. People will be told, "Hey, Jesus has forgiven all your sins! Now stop mourning them!" This is like immediately telling a man whose spouse has died, "Hey, Jesus has taken your wife to heaven! Now stop mourning her death!" That may be a well-meaning thing to do, but in the case of persons who need to grieve, such exhortations are ill-thought-out and can even be harmful.

Of course, if a person mourns too much for his sins and fixates on them, he must be persuaded to snap out of it, just as a man who mourns too long for his wife and fixates on her death must be encouraged to get on with his life. But the point is that this must not be done right after her death. In the same way, a person must not be told to stop mourning for his sins right after he has repented of them. To do so shuts down a needed psychological process, the mourning of a tragedy, one that even Jesus himself underwent when he witnessed or contemplated tragedies (though, being without sin, no tragedies were his fault).

For all of these reasons we can see how, even though Christ's atonement was more than enough to cover both the temporal and the eternal consequences of our sins, we still have a need to mourn our sins; God still often leaves in place a temporal punishment even when he has remitted the eternal one (for example, to teach us our lesson); and we still need to have fellowship restored with God even when we are in a state of forgiveness. The discipline of penance allows us to pursue these things.

This discipline has been recognized by God's people throughout the ages. The system of penance goes back beyond the Middle Ages, through the patristic age, through the New Testament, and into the Old Testament. It has been part of the religion of the one, true God since before the time of Christ, it was part of the religion of Christ and his first followers, and it has been part of Christianity ever since. It was not until the rise of Protestantism that anyone in Christendom thought to deny it. As always, a few pertinent quotations will help to document this fact. Virtually nobody who has read the Old Testament will deny that the ancient Jews did acts of penance—external expressions of sorrow and reparation for sins—as part of their spiritual discipline. Thus we read in words written before the time of Christ:

> Then all the people of Israel, the whole army, went up and came to Bethel and *wept*; they sat there before the LORD, and *fasted* that day until evening, and offered burnt offerings and peace offerings before the LORD [Judg. 20:26].

> Then Jehoshaphat feared, and set himself to seek the LORD, and *proclaimed a fast* throughout all Judah. And Judah assembled to seek help from the LORD; from all the cities of Judah they came to seek the LORD [2 Chron. 20:3–4].

> Then I *proclaimed a fast* there, at the river Ahava, that we might humble ourselves before our God, to seek from him a straight way

for ourselves, our children, and all our goods. For I was ashamed to ask the king for a band of soldiers and horsemen to protect us against the enemy on our way; since we had told the king, "The hand of our God is for good upon all that seek him, and the power of his wrath is against all that forsake him." So we *fasted* and besought our God for this, and he listened to our entreaty [Ezra 8:21–23].

Then I turned my face to the Lord God, seeking him by prayer and supplications with *fasting and sackcloth and ashes* [Dan. 9:3].

Especially informative are passages in which God himself or his prophet commands or rewards fasting or other penance. Such passages as the following show that the practice of penance has God's endorsement:

And when Ahab heard those words, he rent his clothes, and put sackcloth upon his flesh, and fasted and lay in sackcloth, and went about dejectedly. And the word of the LORD came to Elijah the Tishbite, saying, "Have you seen how Ahab has humbled himself before me? Because he has humbled himself before me, I will not bring the evil in his days; but in his son's days I will bring the evil upon his house" [1 Kgs. 21:27–29].

In that day the Lord God of hosts called [you] to weeping and mourning, to baldness and girding with sackcloth; and behold, [instead you engaged in] joy and gladness, slaying oxen and killing sheep, eating flesh and drinking wine [Is. 22:12–13].

Gird on sackcloth and lament, O priests, wail, O ministers of the altar. Go in, pass the night in sackcloth, O ministers of my God! Because cereal offering and drink offering are withheld from the house of your God. Sanctify a fast, call a solemn assembly. Gather the elders and all the inhabitants of the land to the house of the LORD your God; and cry to the LORD [Joel 1:13–14].

"Yet even now," says the LORD, "return to me with all your heart, with fasting, with weeping, and with mourning. . . ." Blow the trumpet in Zion; sanctify a fast; call a solemn assembly [Joel 2:12, 15].

It is also instructive when God explains the purpose of fasting as a means of humbling oneself before him. Evangelicals often have a hard time understanding the reason for fasting. I remember when I was a conservative Presbyterian having one (otherwise very sharp) teaching elder tell me that the idea behind fasting was to give yourself more time to pray by skipping a meal. Reading what the Bible has to say about fasting, one realizes how wrong this answer is. The purpose of skipping the meal(s) is not to make more time available for prayer but to humble (or, to put it more bluntly, to humiliate) oneself before the Lord and seek his favor. And of course the idea of fasting and other acts of penance are clearly endorsed in the New Testament:

> And when you fast, do not look dismal, like the hypocrites, for they disfigure their faces that their fasting may be seen by men. Truly, I say to you, they have their reward. But when you fast, anoint your head and wash your face, that your fasting may not be seen by men but by your Father who is in secret; and your Father who sees in secret will reward you [Matt. 6:16–18].

> Now John's disciples and the Pharisees were fasting; and people came and said to him [Jesus], "Why do John's disciples and the disciples of the Pharisees fast, but your disciples do not fast?" And Jesus said to them, "Can the wedding guests fast while the bridegroom is with them? As long as they have the bridegroom with them, they cannot fast. The days will come, when the bridegroom is taken away from them, and then they will fast in that day" [Mark 2:18–20].

> While they were worshiping the Lord and fasting, the Holy Spirit said, "Set apart for me Barnabas and Saul for the work to which I have called them." Then after fasting and praying they laid their hands on them and sent them off [Acts 13:2–3].

> And when they had appointed elders for them in every church, with prayer and fasting, they committed them to the Lord in whom they believed [Acts 14:23].

> Draw near to God and he will draw near to you. Cleanse your hands, you sinners, and purify your hearts, you men of double mind. Be wretched and mourn and weep. Let your laughter be turned to mourning and your joy to dejection. Humble yourselves before the Lord and he will exalt you [Jas. 4:8–10].

> And I will grant my two witnesses power to prophesy for one
> thousand two hundred and sixty days, clothed in sackcloth [Rev.
> 11:3].

Protestants often skim over the above verses without taking their implications seriously. This is shown especially in sermons on the passage from James. Protestant pastors often tell their congregations to humble themselves before the Lord so that they will be lifted up, but they rob the self-humbling (self-humiliation) of all its content because they *fail* to tell the congregations to humble themselves in the way James has indicated: "grieve, mourn, and wail; change your laughter into mourning and your joy into gloom."

Instead believers are told they don't need to humble themselves in this way because they have already been forgiven by Christ; unbelievers are told they don't need to humble themselves before the Lord in this way because all they have to do is say and believe a prayer and Jesus will take away from them all need of mourning and weeping over their sins. The way this passage is normally preached in Protestant circles, the only people who need to wail and mourn are those who *don't* repent and thus *don't* humiliate themselves before God. The minute a person repents and humbles himself, in a typical Evangelical church he is told he *doesn't* need to do any of the weeping and mourning and wailing James tells him to do as part of his self-humbling.

Of course, if we find the penitential discipline in the Old Testament and the New Testament, it goes without saying that it is found throughout the patristic age. Thus about A.D. 70, the *Didache* tells us: "Before the baptism, let the one baptizing and the one to be baptized fast, as also any others who are able. Command the one who is to be baptized to fast beforehand for one or two days. . . . [After becoming a Christian] do not let your fasts be with the hypocrites. They fast on Monday and Thursday, but you shall fast on Wednesday and Friday" (*Didache* 7:1, 8:1).

About A.D. 80, Pope Clement I tells the Corinthian rebels, "You, therefore, who laid the foundation of the rebellion [in your church], submit to the presbyters and be chastened to repentance, bending your knees in a spirit of humility" (*Letter to the Corinthians* 57).

About A.D. 110, Ignatius of Antioch writes: "For as many as are of God and of Jesus Christ are also with the bishop. And as many as shall, in the exercise of penance, return into the unity of the Church, these, too, shall belong to God, that they may live according to Jesus Christ" (*Letter to the Philadelphians* 3).

About A.D. 203, Tertullian records the practice of Christians and says that "in regard to days of fast, many do not think they should be present at the sacrificial prayers [at the Eucharist], because their fast would be broken if they were to receive the Body of the Lord. Does the Eucharist, then, obviate a work devoted to God, or does it bind it more to God? Will not your fast be more solemn if, in addition, you have stood at God's altar? The Body of the Lord having been received and reserved, each point is secured: both the participation in the sacrifice and the discharge of duty [concerning fasting]" (*Prayer* 19:1–4).

About A.D. 253, Cyprian of Carthage writes that "sinners may do penance for a set time, and according to the rules of discipline come to public confession, and by imposition of the hand of the bishop and clergy receive the right of Communion" (*Letters* 9:2).

About A.D. 388, Jerome tells us that "if the serpent, the devil, bites someone secretly, he infects that person with the venom of sin. And if the one who has been bitten keeps silence and does not do penance, and does not want to confess his wound . . . then his brother and his master, who have the word [of absolution] that will cure him, cannot very well assist him" (*Commentary on Ecclesiastes* 10:11).

Just before A.D. 395, Augustine instructs his catechumens with these words: "When you shall have been baptized, keep to a good life in the commandments of God so that you may preserve your baptism to the very end. I do not tell you that you will live here without sin, but they are venial sins, which this life is never without. Baptism was instituted for all sins. For light sins, without which we cannot live, prayer was instituted. . . . But do not commit those sins on account of which you would have to be separated from the body of Christ. Perish the thought! For those whom you see [at the church] doing penance have committed crimes, either adultery or some other enormities. That is why they are doing penance. If their sins were light, daily prayer would suffice to blot them out. . . . In the Church, therefore, there are three ways in which sins are forgiven: in baptism, in prayer, and in the greater humility of penance" (*Sermon to Catechumens on the Creed* 7:15, 8:16).

So, as we can see, the practice of penance has been part of the true religion since before the time of Christ, at the time of Christ, and after the time of Christ, unchallenged until the time of the Protestant Reformers.

# 5

# Indulgences

The subject of indulgences is certainly one of the most misunderstood aspects of Catholic doctrine. Before beginning to discuss the subject, we should probably set aside a number of common myths concerning the topic.

## Myths about Indulgences

*Myth 1: A person can buy his way out of hell with indulgences.*

This is one of the most common myths that anti-Catholic commentators take advantage of, relying on the ignorance of both Catholics and non-Catholics. But the charge is without foundation. As we will see below, indulgences remit only temporal penalties; they cannot remit the eternal penalty of hell. Once a person is in hell, no number of indulgences will ever change that fact. The only way to avoid hell is by appealing to God's mercy while still alive. After death, one's eternal fate is set (see Heb. 9:27).

*Myth 2: A person can buy indulgences for sins not yet committed.*

Again, false. And most emphatically so! The Church has always taught that indulgences do not apply to sins not yet committed. The 1910 *Catholic Encyclopedia* (s.v. "Indulgences") notes that an indulgence "is not a permission to commit sin, nor a pardon of future sin; neither could be granted by any power."

*Myth 3: A person can buy forgiveness with indulgences.*

The definition of indulgences presupposes that forgiveness has already taken place: "An indulgence is a remission before God of the temporal punishment due to sins whose guilt has already been forgiven" (*Indulgentiarum Doctrina*, norm 1). Indulgences in no way forgive sins. They deal only with temporal consequences left after sins have been forgiven.

*Myth 4: Indulgences were invented to make money for the Church.*

Indulgences developed from reflection on the sacrament of reconciliation. They are a way of shortening the penance of sacramental discipline and were in use centuries before money-related problems appeared.

*Myth 5: An indulgence will shorten one's time in purgatory by a fixed number of days.*

The number of days that formerly were attached to indulgences referred to the period of penance one might undergo during life on earth. The Catholic Church does not teach anything about how long or short purgatory is in general, much less in a specific person's case. Indeed, from a temporal perspective, purgatory may be instantaneous. In such a case, indulgences could affect its intensity but not its temporal duration.

*Myth 6: A person today can buy indulgences.*

The Council of Trent instituted severe reforms in the practice of granting indulgences, and because of prior abuses, "in 1567 Pope Pius V canceled all grants of indulgences involving any fees or other financial transactions" (*Catholic Encyclopedia*, loc. cit.) This act proved the Church's seriousness about removing abuses from indulgences.

*Myth 7: A person formerly could buy indulgences.*

One never could buy indulgences. The financial scandal surrounding indulgences involved alms-indulgences, in which the giving of alms to a charitable fund was used as the occasion to grant the indulgence. The practice was the same in principle as modern nonprofit organizations' granting premium gifts in thanks for donations. That is not the same as selling.

The general purpose of granting indulgences was to encourage people to do spiritually good things and to grow spiritually. The indulgence was an incentive along those lines. Only one kind of indulgence involved alms, and that in itself is an innocent thing. The *Catholic Encyclopedia* notes in its article on indulgences: "Among the good works which might be encouraged by being made the condition of an indulgence, almsgiving would naturally hold a conspicuous place. . . . It is well to observe that in these purposes there is nothing essentially evil. To give money to God or to the poor is a praiseworthy act, and, when it is done from right motives, it will surely not go unrewarded."

## Indulgences Today

Many individuals today, Protestant or Catholic, feel uncomfortable with the topic of indulgences. Some even question whether indulgences are part of the Catholic Church's official teaching. The answer is that they are, though they are not a large part. Of the 2,865 paragraphs in the *Catechism of the Catholic Church*, exactly ten (1471–1479 and 1498) are devoted to the subject of indulgences. This is a rather modest figure, and it accurately reflects the place of indulgences in the hierarchy of truths. The theological principles underlying indulgences are solid, but indulgences are very far from being the most important of the Church's teachings. So it is odd that they attract so much attention from anti-Catholics. Indulgences seem to loom large in the anti-Catholic imagination, and they are the focus of a disproportionate number of the attacks made on the Church.

In responding to these attacks, because of the complexity of explaining the principles behind indulgences to a person hostile to them, some might be tempted to dismiss indulgences as something that one does not have to believe as a Catholic, but this would be a mistake. The Council of Trent infallibly defined that the Church does have the power to grant indulgences.[1] And this was not the first time an ecumenical council had discussed the subject—that was in 1415, when the Council of Constance affirmed the practice —but at Trent the doctrine was proclaimed infallibly for the first time.

## The Principles behind Indulgences

The principles behind indulgences were employed by the Church for centuries before the controversy over them erupted in the 1500s. Indeed, the principles are found in the Bible itself. Catholics who are uncomfortable with indulgences do not realize how biblical they are. The principles behind them are as clear in Scripture as those supporting more familiar (and more important) doctrines, such as the Trinity.

Before looking at those principles more closely, a definition is needed. In his apostolic constitution on indulgences, Pope Paul VI gave this definition:

> An indulgence is a remission before God of the temporal punishment due to sins whose guilt has already been forgiven, which the faithful Christian who is duly disposed gains under certain defined conditions through the Church's help when, as a minister of redemption, she dispenses and applies with authority the treasury of the satisfactions won by Christ and the saints [*Indulgentiarum Doctrina*, norm 1].

---

[1] Trent, session 25, *Decree on Indulgences*.

This technical definition can be phrased more simply: An indulgence is the Church's lessening of the temporal penalties to which we may be subject even though our sins have been forgiven. To understand this definition, we need to look at the biblical principles involved.

*Principle 1: Sin results in guilt and punishment.*

When a person sins, he acquires certain liabilities: the liability of guilt and the liability of punishment.[2] Scripture speaks of the former when it pictures guilt as clinging to our souls, making them discolored and unclean before God: "Come now, let us reason together, says the Lord: Though your sins are like scarlet, they shall be white as snow; though they are red like crimson, they shall become like wool" (Is. 1:18).

This idea of guilt clinging to our souls appears in texts that picture forgiveness as a cleansing or washing and the state of our forgiven souls as clean and white: "Wash me thoroughly from my iniquity, and cleanse me from my sin! . . . Purge me with hyssop, and I shall be clean; wash me, and I shall be whiter than snow" (Ps. 51:2, 7).[3]

We also incur, not just guilt, but liability for punishment when we sin: "I will punish the world for its evil, and the wicked for their iniquity; I will put an end to the pride of the arrogant and lay low the haughtiness of the ruthless" (Is. 13:11). Judgment pertains even to the smallest sins. In Ecclesiastes, we learn that "God will bring every deed into judgment, with every secret thing, whether good or evil" (12:14).[4]

---

[2] The Latin terms for these liabilities are *reatus culpae* and *reatus poena.*

[3] See also Eph. 5:26–27, Acts 22:16, 1 Cor. 6:11, 1 John 1:7, and Rev. 7:13–14.

[4] See also Matt. 12:36 and Rom. 2:16.

*Principle 2: Punishments are both temporal and eternal.*

The Bible indicates that some punishments are eternal, lasting forever, but others are temporal, lasting only for a time. Eternal punishment is mentioned in Daniel 12:2: "And many of those who sleep in the dust of the earth shall awake, some to everlasting life and some to shame and everlasting contempt."[5]

We normally focus on the eternal penalties of sin because they are the most important, but Scripture indicates temporal penalties are real. For example, in Deuteronomy, Moses warns the people:

> If you are not careful to do all the words of this law which are written in this book, that you may fear this glorious and awful name, the LORD your God, then the LORD will bring on you and your offspring extraordinary afflictions, afflictions severe and lasting, and sicknesses grievous and lasting. And he will bring upon you again all the diseases of Egypt, which you were afraid of; and they shall cleave to you. Every sickness also, and every affliction which is not recorded in the book of this law, the LORD will bring upon you, until you are destroyed [Deut. 28:58–61].

Scripture is filled with accounts of temporal punishments being sent on account of sin. While it is important to recognize that not all worldly distress we encounter is produced by our own personal sins (that being the main point of the book of Job), we must recognize the biblical truth that God does allow us to experience temporal as well as eternal calamity on account of our misdeeds.

*Principle 3: Temporal penalties may remain when a sin is forgiven.*

When someone repents, God removes guilt ("Though your sins are like scarlet, they shall be as white as snow" [Is. 1:18]) and any eternal punishment ("Since . . . we are now justified by his blood, much more shall we be saved by him from the wrath of God" [Rom. 5:9]), but temporal penalties may remain. One passage

---

[5] See also Matt. 21:2, 2 Thess. 1:9, and Rev. 14:11.

demonstrating this is 2 Samuel 12, in which Nathan the prophet confronts David over his adultery:

> David said to Nathan, "I have sinned against the LORD." And Nathan said to David, "The LORD also has put away your sin; you shall not die. Nevertheless, because by this deed you have utterly scorned the LORD, the child that is born to you shall die" [2 Sam. 12:13–14].

God forgave David to the point of sparing his life, but David still had to suffer the loss of his son as well as other temporal punishments.[6]

In Numbers we read:

> But Moses said to the LORD, ". . . Now if thou dost kill this people as one man, then the nations who have heard thy fame will say, 'Because the LORD was not able to bring this people into the land which he swore to give to them, therefore he has slain them in the wilderness.' . . ." Then the LORD said, "I have pardoned, according to your word; but truly, as I live . . . none of the men who . . . have not hearkened to my voice, shall see the land which I swore to give to their fathers" [Num. 14:13–23].

God states that, although he pardoned the people, he would impose a temporal penalty by keeping them from the promised land. Later, Moses, who is clearly one of the saved (see Matt. 17:1–5), is told he will suffer a temporal penalty: "And the Lord said to Moses and Aaron, 'Because you did not believe in me, to sanctify me in the eyes of the people of Israel, therefore you shall not bring this assembly into the land which I have given them'" (Num. 20:12; cf. 27:12–14).

Protestants often deny that temporal penalties remain after forgiveness of sin, but they acknowledge in practice that they do —for instance, when they insist on people returning things they have stolen. Thieves may obtain forgiveness, but they also must engage in restitution. Protestants recognize that while Jesus paid the price for our sins before God, he did not relieve our obligation

---

[6] See 2 Sam. 12:7–12 for a list.

to repair the harm we have done. They fully acknowledge that if you steal someone's car, you have to give it back; it isn't enough just to repent. God's forgiveness (and man's!) does not include letting you keep the stolen car.

A Protestant might say that God gives temporal penalties to teach a sinner a lesson, making the penalties discipline rather than punishment. There are three responses to this: (1) Nothing in the above texts says they are discipline rather than punishments; (2) a Catholic could also call them discipline;[7] and (3) there is nothing wrong with calling them punishments, since "disciplining" a child is synonymous in normal speech with punishing a child.

The Catholic has good grounds for claiming that temporal penalties may remain after a sin is forgiven. The Church has shown this since its earliest centuries and prescribed acts of penance as part of the sacrament of reconciliation.

*Principle 4: God blesses some people as a reward to others.*

Suppose a father prays for his seriously ill son, saying, "Dear Lord, if I have pleased you, then please heal my son!" The father is asking that his son be healed as a reward for his (the father's) having pleased God. Intuitively we recognize this as a valid prayer that God sometimes answers positively. But we do not need to stop with our intuitions; Scripture confirms the fact.

After Abraham fought a battle for the Lord, God appeared to him in a vision and said:

> "Fear not, Abram [i.e., Abraham], I am your shield; your reward shall be very great." But Abram said, "O Lord GOD, what wilt thou give me, for I continue childless, and the heir of my house is Eliezer of Damascus?" . . . And behold, the word of the LORD came to him, "This man shall not be your heir; your own son

---

[7] Teaching on indulgences, Pope Paul VI stated that "the punishments with which we are concerned here are imposed by God's judgment, which is just and merciful. The reasons for their imposition are that our souls need to be purified, the holiness of the moral order needs to be strengthened, and God's glory must be restored to its full majesty" (*Indulgentiarum Doctrina* 2).

shall be your heir." And he brought him outside and said, "Look toward heaven, and number the stars, if you are able to number them." Then he said to him, "So shall your descendants be." And he believed the Lord, and he reckoned it to him as righteousness [Gen. 15:1–6].

God promised Abraham a reward—a multitude of descendants who otherwise would not be born. These people received a great gift, the gift of life, because God rewarded the patriarch.

God further told Abraham that he would have nations and kings come from him, that God would make a covenant with his descendants, and that they would inherit the promised land (Gen. 17:6–8). All these blessings came to Abraham's descendants as God's reward to him.

This principle is also present in the New Testament, as we will see in our discussion of Romans 11:28 in the next section. The principle is also found in passages in which one person approaches Jesus for the healing or exorcism of someone else, such as the story of the Canaanite woman (Matt. 15:22–28).

*Principle 5: God remits temporal penalties suffered by some as a reward to others.*

When God blesses one person as a reward to someone else, sometimes the specific blessing he gives is a reduction of the temporal penalties to which the first person is subject. For example, Solomon's heart was led astray from the Lord toward the end of his life, and God promised to rip the kingdom away from him as a result:

Therefore the LORD said to Solomon: "Since this has been your mind and you have not kept my covenant and my statutes which I have commanded you, I will surely tear the kingdom from you and give it to your servant. Yet for the sake of David your father, I will not do it in your days, but I will tear it out of the hand of your son. However I will not tear away all the kingdom; but I will give one tribe to your son for the sake of David my servant and for the sake of Jerusalem which I have chosen" [1 Kgs. 11:11–13].

God lessened the temporal punishment in two ways: by deferring the removal of the kingdom until the days of Solomon's son and by leaving one tribe (Benjamin) under Judah.

God was clear about why he did this: It is not for Solomon's sake, but "for the sake of David your father." If David had not pleased God, and if God had not promised him certain things regarding his kingdom, God would have removed the entire kingdom from Solomon and done so during Solomon's lifetime. This is an example of God's lessening a punishment for the sake of one of his saints.

Other examples are easy to think of. God promised Abraham that if he could find a certain number of righteous men in Sodom, he was willing to defer the city's temporal (and eternal) destruction for the sake of the righteous (Gen. 18:16–33).

Also, Paul noted that "as regards the gospel they [non-Christian Jewish people] are enemies of God, for your sake; but as regards election they are beloved for the sake of their forefathers. For the gifts and the call of God are irrevocable" (Rom. 11:28–29). Paul indicated that his Jewish contemporaries were treated more gently than they otherwise would have been treated (God's gift and call were not removed from them) because their forefathers were beloved by God, who gave them the irrevocable gifts listed in Romans 9:4–5.

*Principle 6: God remits temporal punishments through the Church.*

God uses the Church when he removes temporal penalties. This is a key point in the doctrine of indulgences. The members of the Church became aware of this principle through the sacrament of penance. From the beginning, acts of penance were assigned as part of the sacrament because the Church recognized that Christians must deal with temporal penalties, such as God's discipline and the need to compensate those whom our sins have injured.

In the early Church, acts of penance were sometimes severe. For grave sins, such as apostasy, murder, and abortion, the penance could stretch over years, but the Church recognized that repentant sinners could shorten their penance by pleasing God through pious or charitable acts that expressed sorrow and a desire to make amends for what they had done.

The Church also recognized that the duration of temporal punishments could be lessened through the involvement of other persons who had pleased God (principle 5). Sometimes a confessor[8] or someone soon to be martyred would intervene and ask, as a personal reward, that the penitent have his time of discipline lessened. Thus the Church recognized its role of administrating temporal penalties (principle 6); the role was simply part of the ministry of forgiveness God had given the Church in general.

Scripture tells us that God gave the authority to forgive sins "to men" (Matt. 9:8) and to Christ's ministers in particular. Jesus told them, "As the Father has sent me, even so I send you. . . . Receive the Holy Spirit. If you forgive the sins of any, they are forgiven; if you retain the sins of any, they are retained" (John 20:21–23).

If Christ gave his ministers the ability to forgive the eternal penalty of sin, how much more would they be able to remit the temporal penalties of sin![9] Christ also promised his Church the power to bind and loose on earth: "Truly, I say to you, whatever you bind on earth shall be bound in heaven, and whatever you loose on earth shall be loosed in heaven" (Matt. 18:18). As the context makes clear, binding and loosing cover Church discipline, and Church discipline involves administering and removing temporal penalties (such as barring from and readmitting to the sacra-

---

[8] Here confessors are not priests who hear confessions but those who confessed the Christian faith before the state during a persecution. Confessors, like martyrs, pleased God in a special way by holding to their faith at the risk of their lives.

[9] This kind of argument, of the form "If X is the case, then how much more is Y the case," is called an *a fortiori* argument. *A fortiori* arguments were favorites of Jesus and Paul: See Matt. 7:11, 10:25, 12:12; Luke 11:13, 12:24, 28; Rom. 11:12, 24 and 1 Cor. 6:3; cf. Heb. 9:14.

ments). Therefore, the power of binding and loosing includes the administration of temporal penalties.

*Principle 7: God blesses departed Christians as a reward to living Christians.*

From the beginning, the Church recognized the validity of praying for the dead so that their transition into heaven might be swift and smooth. This meant praying for the lessening or removal of temporal penalties holding them back from the full glory of heaven.

If it is reasonable to ask that these penalties be removed in general, then it would be reasonable to ask that they be removed in a particular case as a reward. A widower could pray to God, asking that if he has pleased God, his wife's transition into glory be hastened. For this reason the Church teaches that "indulgences can always be applied to the dead by way of prayer."[10]

A close parallel to this application is found in 2 Maccabees. Judah Maccabee finds the bodies of soldiers who died wearing superstitious amulets during one of the Lord's battles. Judah and his men "turned to prayer, beseeching that the sin which had been committed might be wholly blotted out" (12:42).

The words "wholly blotted out" refer to the sin's temporal penalties. The author of 2 Maccabees tells us in verse 45 that for these men Judah "was looking to the splendid reward that is laid up for those who fall asleep in godliness"; he believed that these men fell asleep in godliness, which would not have been the case if they were in mortal sin. If they were not in mortal sin, they would not have eternal penalties to suffer, and thus the complete blotting out of their sin must refer to temporal penalties for their superstitious actions. Judah "took up a collection, man by man, to the amount of two thousand drachmas of silver, and sent it to Jerusalem to provide for a sin offering. In doing this . . . he made atonement for the dead, that they might be delivered from their sin" (vv. 43, 45).

---

[10] *Indulgentiarum Doctrina* 3.

Judah not only prayed for the dead but provided for them the then-appropriate action for lessening temporal penalties: a sin offering.[11] Accordingly, we may take the now-appropriate actions for lessening temporal penalties—obtaining indulgences or having Mass offered for a specific person's intention—and apply them to the dead by way of prayer.

There is a difference between the way indulgences are obtained by us in this life and the way they are applied to the dead. The official documents of the Church, such as Pope Paul VI's apostolic constitution on indulgences, the *Code of Canon Law*, and the *Catechism of the Catholic Church*, all note that indulgences are applied to the dead by way of prayer. This is because Christians in the hereafter are no longer under the earthly Church's jurisdiction. They no longer can receive sacraments, including penance, and the Church does not have authority to release their temporal penalties. All it can do is look to God and pray that he will lessen them. This is a valid form of prayer, as 2 Maccabees indicates. We may have confidence that God will apply indulgences to the dead in some way, but the precise manner and degree of application are unknown.[12]

These seven biblical principles are the underpinnings of indulgences, but there are still questions to be asked that may help clarify matters:

*Who are the parties involved in an indulgence?*

There are four parties: The first pleases God and moves him to issue a reward, providing the basis for the indulgence; the second requests the indulgence and obtains it by performing the act pre-

---

[11] The Old Testament sin sacrifices dealt only with the temporal atonement for sins, "for it is impossible that the blood of bulls and goats should take away [the eternal punishment for] sins" (Heb. 10:4).

[12] This is one reason the Church cannot simply "empty purgatory," as Martin Luther suggested it should. Because it lacks jurisdiction, the earthly Church can only pray for those there.

scribed for it; the third issues the indulgence (this is God working through the Church); and the fourth receives the benefit of the indulgence by having his temporal penalties lessened.[13]

*How many of one's temporal penalties can be remitted?*

Potentially, all of them. The Church recognizes that Christ and the saints are interested in helping penitents deal with the aftermath of their sins, as indicated by the fact that they pray for us (Heb. 7:25, Rev. 5:8). Fulfilling its role in the administration of temporal penalties, the Church draws upon the rewards God chose to bestow on the saints, who pleased him, and on his Son, who pleased him most of all.[14]

---

[13] Some parties may be one and the same person. The person who provides the basis for an indulgence may request one and apply it to another; the person who requests an indulgence may ask it for himself or someone else. But one limit under current canon law is that one may not obtain an indulgence for another living person (although it is possible to do so in principle, as the case of the early penitents shows).

[14] These rewards are metaphorically referred to as "the treasury of the Church," or sometimes as "the treasury of merits." A merit is anything that pleases God and moves him to issue a reward, not things that earn "payment" from God. Human beings can't earn anything from God, though by his grace they can please him in a way he chooses to reward. Picturing the saints' acts under a single, collective metaphor (such as a treasury) is biblical: "It was granted her [the Bride] to be clothed with fine linen, bright and pure" (Rev. 19:8). John, the author of Revelation, tells us that "the fine linen is the righteous deeds of the saints." Here the righteous deeds of the saints are pictured under the collective metaphor of clothing on the Bride of Christ, the Church. Jewish theology also recognizes a treasury of merits. Jewish theologians speak of "the merits of the fathers"—the idea being that the patriarchs pleased God and inherited certain promises as a reward. God fulfills these promises and ends up treating later Jews more gently than they would have been treated otherwise. The idea of "the merits of the fathers" is essentially the same as the Catholic concept of the "treasury of the Church." Both postulate a class of individuals, the Old Testament patriarchs on the one hand and Christ and the saints on the other, who have pleased God and whom God chooses to reward in a way involving lesser temporal punishments for others.

The rewards on which the Church draws are infinite because Christ is God, so the rewards he accrued are infinite and never can be exhausted. His rewards alone, apart from the saints', could remove all temporal penalties from everyone, everywhere. The rewards of the saints are added to Christ's, not because anything is lacking in his, but because God has chosen to associate man with the application of salvation, as we saw in chapters 2 and 3.

*If the Church has the resources to wipe out everyone's temporal penalties, why doesn't it do so?*

First, because God does not wish this to be done. God himself instituted the pattern of temporal penalties being left after forgiveness. They fulfill valid functions, one of them disciplinary. If a child were never disciplined, he would never learn obedience. God disciplines us as his children: "For the Lord disciplines him whom he loves, and chastises every son whom he receives" (Heb. 12:6). So some temporal penalties must remain.

Second, the Church *cannot* wipe out, with a stroke of the pen, so to speak, everyone's temporal punishments because their remission depends on the dispositions of the persons who suffer those temporal punishments. Just as repentance and faith are needed for the remission of eternal penalties, so they are needed for the remission of temporal penalties. As Pope Paul VI explained, "Indulgences cannot be gained without a sincere conversion of outlook and unity with God." [15] We might say that the degree of remission depends on how well the penitent has learned his lesson.

*How does one determine by what amount penalties have been lessened?*

Before Vatican II each indulgence was reckoned as removing a certain number of "days" from one's discipline. For instance, an act might gain "300 days indulgence"—but the use of the term *days* confused people, giving them the mistaken impression that in purgatory time operates as it does here and that we can calculate "time off in purgatory" in a mechanical way. The number

---

[15] *Indulgentiarum Doctrina* 11.

of days associated with indulgences never literally meant that the indicated amount of time would be taken off one's stay in purgatory. Instead, it meant that an indefinite but partial amount of remission would be granted, proportionate to what ancient Christians would have received for performing that many days' penance. So, someone gaining 300 days indulgence gained roughly what an early Christian would have gained by, say, reciting a particular prayer on arising for 300 days.

To overcome the confusion, Paul VI changed the system. Today, numbers of days are not associated with indulgences. Instead, they are classified as either plenary or partial. Only God knows for certain exactly how efficacious any particular partial indulgence is or whether a plenary indulgence was received when there was the opportunity for one.

*Do indulgences duplicate or even negate the work of Christ?*

Despite the biblical underpinnings of indulgences, some are sharply critical of them and insist that the doctrine supplants the work of Christ and turns us into our own saviors. This objection results from misapprehension concerning the nature of indulgences and about how Christ's work is applied to us.

As we have seen, indulgences apply only to temporal penalties, not to eternal ones. The Bible indicates that these penalties may remain after a sin has been forgiven and that God lessens these penalties as rewards to those who have pleased him. Since the Bible indicates this, Christ's work cannot be said to have been supplanted by indulgences. The Church merely acts as Christ's servant in the application of what he has done for us, and we know from Scripture that Christ's work is applied to us over time and not in one big lump (see Phil. 2:12, 1 Pet. 1:9).

*What about the merits of the saints—by the doctrine of indulgences are the saints made co-saviors with Christ?*

They're not eternal saviors. But it is not inappropriate to describe them as saviors in the temporal sense we discussed in chapter 2— i.e., as those who help deliver from temporal difficulties. Being a savior in this way is something any human may do for another without blaspheming Christ.[16]

Further, the role they are able to play in this regard is, from first to last, based on God's grace. The saints have the ability to please God because the love of God has been put in their hearts (Rom. 5:5), but it is only because of God's grace that this is so. His grace produces all their good actions, and his grace is given to them because of what Christ did. The good actions of the saints therefore are produced by Christ's working through them, which means Christ is the ultimate cause of even this temporal salvation.

Most fundamentally, however, the above objection may be met simply by pointing out, as was done in chapter 2, that Scripture uses the word "savior" to talk about ordinary humans as temporal saviors. That in no way undercuts the unique role of Christ as eternal Savior.

*Should we be talking along these lines? Isn't it better to put all of the emphasis on Christ alone?*

No. If we ignore the principles underlying indulgences, we neglect what Christ does through us, and we fail to recognize the value of what he has done in us. Paul used this very sort of language: "Now I rejoice in my sufferings for your sake, and in my flesh I complete what is lacking in Christ's afflictions for the sake of his body, that is, the Church" (Col. 1:24).

Even though Christ's sufferings were far more than needed to pay for everything, Paul spoke of completing what was "lacking" in Christ's sufferings. If this mode of speech was permissible for Paul, it is permissible for us, even though the Catholic language about indulgences is far less shocking to some ears than was Paul's language about his own role in salvation.

---

[16] For example, it does not offend Christ for a fireman to pull a child out of a burning building. The idea of one human saving another from temporal misfortune does not diminish the victory of Christ.

*Catholics sometimes talk about "expiating" sin in connection with indul-
gences. Isn't expiation something only Christ can do?*

Some criticize indulgences by saying that only Christ can make
"expiation" for our sins. While this sounds like a noble defense of
Christ's sufficiency, the criticism is misfounded, and many who
make it do not understand what the word *expiation* means or how
indulgences work.

Protestant Scripture scholar Leon Morris comments on the confusion surrounding the word *expiate.* After noting that most people "don't understand 'expiation' very well," Morris explains that
"expiation is . . . the making amends for a wrong." [17]

The *Wycliff Bible Encyclopedia* gives a similar definition: "The
basic idea of expiation has to do with reparation for a wrong, the
satisfaction of the demands of justice through paying a penalty." [18]
It also notes the same thing that the term has somewhat imper-
sonal connotations. [19]

The terms used in these definitions—*expiation, amends, satisfaction, reparation*—refer basically to the same thing. To make expiation or satisfaction for a sin is to make amends or reparation
for it. When someone makes reparations, he tries to repair the
situation caused by his sin.

Certainly when it comes to the eternal effects of our sins, only
Christ can make amends or reparation. Only he was able to pay
the infinite price necessary for our sins. We are completely unable to do so, not only because we are finite creatures incapable
of making an infinite satisfaction, but also because everything we
have was given to us by God. For us to try to satisfy God's eternal

---

[17] Morris, L., *The Atonement* (Downers Grove: InterVarsity, 1983), 151.

[18] *Wycliff Bible Encyclopedia* (Chicago: Moody, 1975), 1:578.

[19] It explains, for instance, that expiation differs from propitiation, which
"carries in addition the idea of appeasing an offended person, of regaining the
favor of a higher individual" (ibid.). Thus expiation and propitiation both
focus on fixing things after a wrong has been committed, but the former focuses on the wrong itself whereas the latter focuses on the one offended by
the wrong.

justice would be like using money we had borrowed from someone to repay what we had stolen from him. No actual satisfaction
would be made (cf. Ps. 49:7–9, Job 41:11, Rom. 11:35).

This does not mean we cannot make amends or reparation for
the temporal effects of our sins. If someone steals an item, he
can return it. If someone damages another's reputation, he can
publicly correct the slander. When someone destroys a piece of
property, he can compensate the owner for its loss. All these are
ways one can make at least partial amends (expiation) for harm
done.

These are ways in which we are expected to make compensation, as even the sharpest critics of indulgences admit. If I have
wronged another person, then, in addition to getting right with
God, I must make up for my offense, or at least try, to the person
I have wronged. To make full reparation, it is necessary not only
to restore what was taken or damaged but also to compensate the
owner for the time the thing was gone or injured. In financial
cases this is done by paying interest.

Excellent biblical illustrations of this principle are given in
Leviticus 6:1–7 and Numbers 5:5–8, which tell us that in the
Old Testament a penitent had to pay an extra twenty percent in
addition to the value of the thing he took or damaged. (This applied to a penitent who voluntarily made compensation; a cap-
tured thief had to pay back double the value of the item taken
[Ex. 22:7–9].) One of the most significant passages dealing with
this issue is one we have quoted before—Proverbs 16:6: "By loving kindness and faithfulness iniquity is atoned for." Here we are
told that a person makes temporal atonement for his sins through
acts of loving kindness and faithfulness.

In any event, since expiation equals making amends and since
Protestants are agreed that one who has sinned should make
amends as best he can, there can be no objection to the principle of making temporal expiation for one's sins. To dispute this
would be to quarrel about the term, not the doctrine it represents.

In conclusion, Catholics should not be defensive about indulgences. They are based on principles straight from the Bible, and

we can be confident not only that indulgences exist but that they are useful and worth obtaining.

Pope Paul VI declared that "the Church invites all its children to think over and weigh up in their minds as well as they can how the use of indulgences benefits their lives and all Christian society. . . . Supported by these truths, Holy Mother Church again recommends the practice of indulgences to the faithful. It has been very dear to Christian people for many centuries as well as in our own day. Experience proves this."[20]

---

[20] *Indulgentiarum Doctrina* 9, 11.

# 6

# A Tiptoe through TULIP

Because the Bible uses the term predestination,[1] all Christian churches believe in some doctrine of predestination. But what predestination is and how it works are in dispute.

In Protestant circles there are two major camps when it comes to predestination: Calvinism and Arminianism.[2] Calvinism is common in Presbyterian, Reformed, and a few Baptist churches. Arminianism is common in Methodist, Pentecostal, and most Baptist churches.[3]

Even though Calvinists are a minority among Protestants today, their view has had great influence, especially in this country. This is partly because the Puritans and the Baptists who helped found America were Calvinists, but it is also because Calvinism traditionally has been found among the more intellectual Protestants, giving it a special influence.

Calvinists claim that God predestines people by choosing which individuals will accept his offer of salvation. These people are known as "the elect."[4] Calvinists stress that the elect are not

---

[1] See Rom. 8:29–30, Eph. 1:5, 11. For the Church's teaching on predestination see Ludwig Ott, *Fundamentals of Catholic Dogma* (Rockford, Illinois: TAN Books, 1992 reprint ed.), 242–244.

[2] Calvinists are followers of John Calvin (1509–1564). Arminians are followers of Jacob Arminius (1560–1609).

[3] In Catholic circles, the two major groups discussing predestination are the Thomists and the Molinists, followers of Thomas Aquinas (1225–1274) and Luis de Molina (1536–1600). Thomists emphasize the role of grace, while Molinists emphasize free will, but neither school ignores what is emphasized by the other.

[4] From the Greek word *eklektos*, which means "chosen."

saved *against* their will. It is *because* God has chosen them that they will desire to come to him in the first place. Those who are not among the elect, "the reprobate," will not desire to come to God, will not do so, and thus will not be saved.

Calvinists are sometimes wrongly criticized as teaching that a person may as well be unconcerned about his salvation since he is already either among the elect or the reprobate. According to a Calvinist, it would be a mistake for a person to say, "Well, if God chooses me, I'll be saved; if he doesn't, I won't. So I can sit back and do nothing." Calvinists rightly point out that a person who says this until his death shows that he was not one of the elect because he never did the things, such as repenting and trusting God, that are necessary for salvation.

Arminians, by contrast, claim God predestines people by pronouncing (but not deciding) who will accept salvation. He makes this pronouncement using his foreknowledge, which enables him to see what people will do in the future. He sees who will choose freely to accept his offer of salvation. The people who God knows will repent are those he regards as his "elect," or "chosen."

The debate between Calvinists and Arminians is often fierce. They frequently accuse each other of teaching a false gospel, at least on a theoretical level, although on a practical level there is little difference between the two since both groups agree on the practical steps one must take to be saved (i.e., repent, believe the gospel, etc.).[5] The debate is centered on the well-known formula TULIP. Each letter of this acronym stands for a different doctrine held by classical Calvinists[6] but rejected by Arminians:

---

[5] Among Catholics the discussion has been more peaceful. Since the controversy over grace in the late 1500s and early 1600s, Thomists and Molinists have been forbidden to accuse each other of heresy. In 1748 the Church declared Thomism, Molinism, and a third view known as Augustinianism to be acceptable to Catholic teaching.

[6] Some Calvinists, known as Amyraldians or "four-point Calvinists," hold all of TULIP except for L.

| T | = | Total depravity |
|---|---|---|
| U | = | Unconditional election |
| L | = | Limited atonement |
| I | = | Irresistible grace |
| P | = | Perseverance of the saints |

It is important for Catholics to know about these subjects for several reasons. First, Catholics are often attacked by Calvinists who misunderstand the Catholic position on these issues; second, Catholics often misunderstand the teaching of their own Church on predestination; and third, in recent years a large number of Calvinists have become Catholics.[7] By understanding Calvinism better, Catholics can help more Calvinists make the jump.

In looking at the TULIP formula, we will often note places where Catholics may agree with a point of Calvinist theology and a few places where a Catholic must agree (e.g., that we are totally unable to come to God without his grace). There is a distinction between these two, however. Just because a Catholic is free to agree with a position does not mean that he must do so. In this chapter we are concerned with how close a Catholic could get to the Calvinist position without falsifying Catholic theology, so we will be looking at the subject of predestination primarily through a Thomist lens, not primarily through the lenses of other permitted Catholic schools of thought.[8]

## Total Depravity

Despite its name, the doctrine of total depravity does not mean men are always and only sinful. Calvinists do not think we are as sinful as we possibly could be. They claim that our free will

---

[7] Including myself.

[8] I should add that the reader should not assume that my own views are necessarily Thomist. This is not about *my* views but what views can be legitimately held within the bounds of Catholic theology.

has been injured by original sin to the point that unless God gives us special grace, we cannot free ourselves from sin and choose to serve him in charity. We might choose to serve him out of fear or some other motive, but not out of supernatural love.[9]

What would a Catholic think of this teaching? While he would not use the term "total depravity"[10] to describe the doctrine, he would actually agree with it. The accepted Catholic teaching is that, because of the fall of Adam, man cannot do anything out of charity (supernatural love) unless God gives him special grace to do so.[11] Thomas Aquinas declared that special grace is necessary for man to do any supernaturally good act, to love God, to fulfill God's commandments, to gain eternal life, to prepare for salvation, to rise from sin, to avoid sin, and to persevere (ST I-II:109:2-10).

---

[9] Of course, there is nothing wrong with serving out of godly fear. The Bible often uses fear of divine chastisement as a motivator. Love and a certain kind of fear do not exclude each other: a child may both love his parents and have a healthy fear of their discipline. But service based on fear alone does not please God in a supernatural way and does not receive a supernatural reward. Charity is necessary to please God and receive rewards.

[10] This term is badly misleading, as even Calvinists acknowledge. For example, Calvinist theologian R. C. Sproul proposes the alternative term "radical corruption," although this is not much better. Author Loraine Boettner suggests the much better term "total inability" in his book *The Reformed Doctrine of Predestination* (Phillipsburg, New Jersey: P & R Publishing, reprinted 1992).

[11] In *Fundamentals of Catholic Dogma*, Ludwig Ott gives the following as a defined article of faith: "For every salutary act internal supernatural grace of God (*gratia elevans*) is absolutely necessary" (Ott, 229). He goes on to cite the Second Council of Orange, which stated that "as often as we do good God operates in us and with us, so that we may operate" (canon 9) and that "man does no good except that which God brings about" (canon 20). The Council of Trent infallibly *condemned* the proposition that "without the predisposing inspiration of the Holy Ghost and without his help, man can believe, hope, love, or be repentant as he ought, so that the grace of justification may be bestowed upon him" (*Decree on Justification* 3). The Church teaches that God's grace is necessary to enable man to be lifted out of sin, to display genuine supernatural virtues, and to please God.

## *Unconditional Election*

The doctrine of unconditional election means that God does not base his choice (election) of certain individuals on anything other than his own good will.[12] God chooses whomever he pleases and passes over the rest. The ones God chooses will desire to come to him, will accept freely his offer of salvation, and will do so precisely because he has chosen them.

To show that God positively chooses rather than merely foresees those who will come to him, Calvinists cite passages such as Romans 9:15–18, in which the Lord "says to Moses, 'I will have mercy on whom I have mercy, and I will have compassion on whom I have compassion.' So it depends not upon man's will or exertion, but upon God's mercy. . . . So then he has mercy upon whomever he wills, and he hardens the heart of whomever he wills."[13]

What would a Catholic say about this? Certainly Catholics are free to disagree with the Calvinist interpretation, but they are also free to agree. All Thomists and even some Molinists (such as Robert Bellarmine and Francisco Suarez) taught unconditional election. Thomas Aquinas says this:

> God wills to manifest his goodness in men: in respect to those whom he predestines, by means of his mercy, in sparing them; and in respect of others, whom he reprobates, by means of his justice, in punishing them. This is the reason why God elects some and rejects others. . . . Yet why he chooses some for glory and reprobates others has no reason except the divine will. Hence Augustine says, "Why he draws one, and another he draws not, seek not to judge, if thou dost not wish to err" [ST I:23:5, citing Augustine's *Homilies on the Gospel of John* 26:2].

---

[12] The Arminians assert that God bases his choice on his knowledge of what individuals will do in the future.

[13] *Contra* Calvinism, one may understand this hardening in terms of Rom. 1:20–32, where Paul repeatedly states that God gave pagans up to their sinful desires after they refused to acknowledge him. See also Jas. 1:13.

Although a Catholic may agree with unconditional election, he may not affirm "double predestination," a doctrine Calvinists often infer from it. This teaching claims that in addition to electing some people to salvation, God also actively chooses others to be damned.

The alternative to double predestination is to say that while God predestines some people, he simply passes over the remainder. They will not come to God, but it is because of their own sin, not because God actively chooses them for damnation. This is the doctrine of passive reprobation, which Aquinas taught (ST I:23:3).

The Council of Trent firmly and infallibly rejected the propositions (1) "that it is not in the power of man to make his ways evil, but that God produces the evil as well as the good works, not only by permission, but also properly and of himself, so that the betrayal of Judas is no less his own proper work than the vocation of Paul" and (2) "that the grace of justification is attained by those only who are predestined unto life, but that all others, who are called, are called indeed, but do not receive grace, as if they are by divine power predestined to evil."[14]

## Limited Atonement

Calvinists believe the atonement is limited, that Christ offered it for some of us but not for all. They claim Christ died only for the elect. To prove this they cite verses that say Christ died for his sheep (John 10:11), for his friends (John 15:13–14a), and for the Church (Acts 20:28, Eph. 5:25).[15]

---

[14] *Decree on Justification*, canons 6 and 17. The same points were taught by the Second Council of Orange (531), the Council of Quiersy (853), and the Third Council of Valencia (855). Although none of these were ecumenical councils, the canons of II Orange are commonly considered infallible due to their special reception.

[15] Calvinists view these groups as identical with the elect. This assumption

But these verses do not prove Christ died only for the elect. A person may give himself or give of himself for one person or group, but that does not preclude his doing so for others as well.[16] Biblical proof of this principle is found in Galatians 2:20, where Paul says that Christ "loved me and gave himself for me," not at all implying that Christ did not also give himself for other people besides Paul. That Christ is said to have given himself in a special way for his sheep, his friends, or the Church cannot be used to prove that Christ did not also give himself for all men in a different way.

The Bible maintains that there is a sense in which Christ died for all men. John 4:42 describes Christ as "the Savior of the world," and 1 John 2:2 states that Christ "is the propitiation for our sins, and not for ours only but also for the whole world." In 1 Timothy 4:10, God is described as "the Savior of all men, especially of those who believe." These passages, as well as the official teaching of the Church,[17] require the Catholic to affirm that Christ died to atone for all men.

Aquinas taught that "Christ's Passion was not only a sufficient but a superabundant atonement for the sins of the human race; according to 1 John 2:2, 'He is the propitiation for our sins, and not for ours only, but also for those of the whole world'" (ST III:48:2).

This is not to say there is no sense in which limitation may be ascribed to the atonement. While the grace it provided is sufficient to pay for the sins of all men, this grace is not made efficacious in the case of everyone. One may say that although the sufficiency

---

is false. Not all who are at one time Christ's sheep or Christ's friends remain so (see below on perseverance of the saints). Similarly, not all who are in the Church are among the elect.

[16] Suppose, for example, a group of people have been kidnapped. Among them are the friends of a certain rich man. He desires to liberate them, but the kidnappers will only release his friends if they are paid ransom for the group as a whole. The rich man then pays a price sufficient to free all the kidnapping victims, even though he may have done so to liberate his friends in particular.

[17] See Ott, 188f.

of the atonement is not limited, its efficiency is limited. This is something everyone who believes in hell must acknowledge because if the atonement were made efficacious for everyone, no one would end up in hell.

The difference between the atonement's sufficiency and its efficiency accounts for Paul's statement that God is "the Savior of all men, especially of those who believe" (1 Tim. 4:10). God is the Savior of all men because he arranged a sacrifice sufficient for all men. He is the Savior of those who believe in a special and superior sense because these have the sacrifice made efficacious for them. According to Aquinas, Christ is "the propitiation for our sins, efficaciously for some, but sufficiently for all, because the price of his blood is sufficient for the salvation of all; but it has its effect only in the elect."[18]

A Catholic also may say that, in going to the cross, Christ intended to make salvation possible, though not actual, for all men —otherwise we would have to say that Christ went to the cross expecting that all men would end up in heaven. This is clearly not the case.[19] A Catholic therefore may say that the atonement is limited in efficacy, if not in sufficiency, and that God intended it to be this way.[20] While a Catholic cannot say that the atonement is limited in that it was made only for the elect, he can say that the atonement is limited in that God only intended it to be efficacious for the elect (although he intended it to be sufficient for all).[21]

---

[18] *Commentary on Titus* 1:2:6.

[19] Matt. 18:7–9, 22:13, 24:40f., 51, 25:30, Mark 9:48, Luke 3:17, 16:19–31, and especially Matt. 7:13f., 26:24, Luke 13:23ff., and Acts 1:25.

[20] One must be sure to maintain that God desires the salvation of all men, as the Catholic Church teaches. 1 Tim. 2:4 states that God "desires all men to be saved and to come to the knowledge of the truth." See also Ezek. 33:11. This does not necessarily conflict with God's intent to save only some, since a person may desire one thing but intend another. A father may desire not to punish his son, but he may intend to do so nonetheless.

[21] Some Calvinists are unhappy with the statement that the atonement is limited. They prefer saying that Christ made a "particular redemption" rather

## Irresistible Grace

Calvinists teach that when God gives a person the grace to come to salvation, the person always responds and never rejects this grace. For this reason, many have called this the doctrine of irresistible grace. This designation has the drawback of sounding as though God forces people against their will to come to him. The designation also sounds unbiblical, since Scripture indicates that grace can be resisted. In Acts 7:51, Stephen tells the Sanhedrin, "You always resist the Holy Spirit!"[22]

For this reason, many Calvinists are displeased with the phrase "irresistible grace." Some have proposed alternatives. Loraine Boettner, perhaps best known to Catholics as the author of the inflammatory and inaccurate book *Roman Catholicism*, prefers "efficacious grace."[23] The idea is that God's enabling grace is intrinsically efficacious, so it always produces salvation.

This is the principal issue between the two major Catholic schools of thought, Thomists and Molinists.[24] Thomists claim that this enabling grace is intrinsically efficacious: By its very nature, because of the kind of grace it is, it always produces the effect of salvation. Molinists claim that God's enabling grace is only sufficient and is made efficacious by man's free choice rather than by the nature of the grace itself. For this reason, Molinists say that enabling grace is *extrinsically* efficacious rather than *intrinsically* efficacious.[25]

---

than a "limited atonement." These mean the same thing, but since the former destroys the TULIP acrostic, the latter is normally used.

[22] See also Sir. 15:11–20, Matt. 23:37.

[23] Loraine Boettner, op. cit., ch. 8, "Efficacious Grace."

[24] Some Molinists, such as Bellarmine and Suarez, almost have been Thomists. They agree with almost all that Thomism says, such as the affirmation of unconditional election, but they reject the idea that grace is intrinsically efficacious.

[25] One should note that Thomists do believe in free will, although not the sort Molinists believe in. They claim God's grace establishes what will be

A Catholic can agree with the idea that enabling grace is intrinsically efficacious and, consequently, that all who receive this grace will repent and come to God. Aquinas teaches that "God's intention cannot fail. . . . Hence if God intends, while moving it, that the one whose heart he moves should attain to grace, he will infallibly attain to it, according to John 6:45, 'Everyone that has heard and learned from the Father comes to me'" (ST I-II:112:3).

Catholics must say that, though God may give efficacious grace only to some, he gives sufficient grace to all. This is presupposed by the fact that he intended the atonement to be sufficient for all. Vatican II states that "since Christ died for all men, and since the ultimate calling of man is in fact one and divine, we ought to believe that the Holy Spirit in a manner known only to God offers to every man the possibility of being associated with this paschal mystery."[26]

## Perseverance of the Saints

Calvinists teach that a person who enters a state of grace will never leave it but will persevere to the end of life. This doctrine is normally called the "perseverance of the saints."[27] All those who are at any time saints (i.e., in a state of sanctifying grace,

---

freely chosen, but in a way that does not disturb the will's freedom. Aquinas says, "God changes the will without forcing it. But he can change the will from the fact that he himself operates in the will as he does in nature" (*De Veritate* 22:9).

[26] *Gaudium et Spes* 22; "being associated with this paschal mystery" results in being saved.

[27] Many Calvinists prefer the phrase "preservation of the saints," since it puts emphasis on God's preservation of the saints rather than on the saints' efforts in persevering (which is thought to smack of "works-salvation"). This often results in a holier-than-thou attitude ("Look how holy I am; I place the emphasis on *God's* action, not *man's*"). But Scripture normally uses a human point of view. It calls men to repent, have faith, convert, and persevere. When one insists on preservation language over perseverance language, one may find oneself taking a holier-than-Thou attitude, because the One who wrote Scrip-

to use Catholic terminology) will remain so forever. No matter what trials they face, they will always persevere, so their salvation is eternally secure.[28]

Analogies are used to support this teaching. Calvinists point out that when we become Christians, we become God's children. They infer that, just as a child's position in the family is secure, our position in God's family is secure. A father would not kick his son out, so God will not kick us out. This reasoning is faulty. The analogy does not prove what it is supposed to. Children do not have "eternal security" in their families. They can be disowned, and even if a father would not kick anyone out, a child can leave the house on his own, repudiate his parents, and sever all ties with the family. Further, children can die; we, as God's children, can die spiritual deaths after we have been spiritually "born again."[29]

---

ture used perseverance-language more than preservation-language. In effect, one may be playing spiritual one-upmanship with Scripture and the One who wrote Scripture.

[28] This differs from the "once saved, always saved" teaching common in Baptist circles. According to that theory, a person never can lose his salvation, no matter what he does. Even if he leaves the faith and renounces Christ, he will be saved. Perseverance of the saints states that, while a person would lose his salvation *if* he fails to persevere in faith and holiness, all who do come to God in fact will persevere. If a person does not persevere, he did not come to God in the first place. Passages such as 1 Cor. 6:9–10 and Gal. 5:19–21, which say that a person will not inherit the kingdom if he commits certain sins, are understood to mean that one who habitually commits these sins was never a true Christian, no matter how sincere he appeared. Both "once saved, always saved" and perseverance of the saints teach "eternal security," but they are not the same. Calvinism admits there are mortal sins, such as failure to persevere, but says that no one who is saved commits these sins. "Once saved, always saved" says no sin would be mortal for a Christian, even in principle.

[29] Elements of these responses are brought together in Luke 15, where the prodigal son begins as a son, then leaves the family and is spoken of by the father as "dead," only to return to the family and be spoken of as being "alive again" (Luke 15:24, 32). Christ teaches that we can be sons, die spiritually by severing our ties to the family, then come back and be alive again—spiritually resurrected.

Calvinists also use Bible passages to teach perseverance of the saints, chiefly John 6:37–39, 10:27–29, and Romans 8:35–39. The Calvinist interpretation of these passages takes them out of context,[30] and there are numerous other exegetical problems with this interpretation.[31]

Calvinists assume that the idea of predestination entails perseverance of the saints. If one is predestined to be saved, does it not follow that one must persevere to the end? This assumption involves a confusion about what people are predestined *to*: initial salvation or final salvation. The two are not the same. A person may be predestined to one but not necessarily to the other.[32] One must define which kind of predestination is being discussed.

If one is talking about predestination to initial salvation, a person's coming to God does not of itself mean he will stay with God. If one is talking about predestination to final salvation, then a predestined person will stay with God, but this does not mean the predestined are the *only* ones who experience initial salvation. Some may genuinely come to God (because they were predestined to initial salvation) and then genuinely leave (because they were

---

[30] John 6:37–39 and 10:27–29 are taken out of context with John 15:1–6, which states that Christians are branches in the vine that is Christ (v. 5), that God removes every branch from Christ that does not bear fruit (v. 2), and that the destiny of these branches is to be burned (v. 6). Rom. 8:35–39 is taken out of context with Rom. 11:20–24, where Paul compares spiritual Israel to an olive tree and states that since certain branches of spiritual Israel were broken off because of unbelief in Christ (v. 20), Christians will not be spared if they fall into unbelief (v. 21), but will be cut off (v. 22). The branches that had been broken off may be grafted on again (vv. 23–24). Rom. 8:35–39 is also taken out of context with Rom. 8:12–13, 17, and 14:15, 20.

[31] For further discussion see Robert Shank, *Life in the Son* (Minneapolis: Bethany House, 1989) and Dale Moody, *The Word of Truth* (Grand Rapids: Eerdmans, 1981), 348ff. Both authors are Baptists who believe in conditional security, not eternal security.

[32] It is clear that being predestined to enter a state—such as the state of grace —does not mean being predestined to remain in it forever. To give a mundane example, if a person were predestined to enter your living room, it would not mean he was predestined to remain there forever.

not predestined to final salvation).[33] Either way, predestination to initial salvation does not entail predestination to final salvation.[34] There is no *logical* reason why a person cannot be predestined to "believe for a while" but "in time of temptation fall away" (Luke 8:13).[35]

A Catholic must affirm that there are people who experience initial salvation yet do not go on to final salvation, but he is free to hold to a form of perseverance of the saints. The question is how one defines the term *saints*—in the Calvinist way, as all those who *ever* enter a state of salvation (i.e., sanctifying grace), or in a more Catholic way, as those who will go on to have their sanctification (their "saintification") completed.[36] If one defines *saint* in the latter sense, a Catholic may believe in perseverance of the saints, since a person predestined to final salvation must by definition persevere to the end. Catholics even have a special name for the grace God gives these people: "the gift of final perseverance."

The Church teaches that there is a gift of final perseverance.[37]

---

[33] Catholic theology typically understands "predestined" to mean "predestined to final salvation." Thus those who will end up with God in heaven are spoken of as "the predestined" or "the elect." That a person experiences salvation at some point does not mean he is among the predestined (i.e., those God has chosen to persevere to the end).

[34] Once the issue of which kind of predestination is being discussed is cleared up, we can evaluate the teaching of Scripture objectively. When we do so, it is clear that there are numerous indications in the Bible that a person can lose salvation. We have already mentioned John 15:1–6, Rom. 8:12f., 17, 11:20–24, and 14:15–20. There are many more. Robert Shank gives a list of eighty-five passages he believes will, if carefully interpreted in context, show that loss of salvation is possible (see Shank, 333–337).

[35] I recognized this fact even as a Calvinist. Though I believed in perseverance of the saints, I recognized that being predestined to come to God did not logically require being predestined to stay with him.

[36] *Sanctification* and *saintification* are the same concept. When one has been completely sanctified (made holy), one has become a saint in the fullest sense of the word. Since this applies only to those in heaven, it corresponds to the common Catholic usage of the term *saint*.

[37] Trent's *Decree on Justification*, canon 16, speaks of "that great and special

Aquinas says (as does Molina) that this grace always ensures that a person will persevere.[38] Aquinas says that "predestination [to final salvation] most certainly and infallibly takes effect" (ST I:23:6).

But not all who come to God receive this grace. Aquinas also teaches that the gift of final perseverance is

> the abiding in good to the end of life. In order to have this perseverance man . . . needs the divine assistance guiding and guarding him against the attacks of the passions. . . . [A]fter anyone has been justified by grace, he still needs to beseech God for the aforesaid gift of perseverance, that he may be kept from evil till the end of life. For to many grace is given to whom perseverance in grace is not given [ST I-II:109:10].

The idea that a person can be predestined to come to God yet not be predestined to stay the course may be new and strange-sounding to Calvinists, but it did not sound new or strange to Augustine, Aquinas, or even Luther. Calvinists frequently cite these men as "Calvinists before Calvin." While holding some similar views of predestination, they did not draw Calvin's inference that all who are ever saved are predestined to remain in grace.[39]

---

gift of final perseverance," and chapter 13 of the decree speaks of "the gift of perseverance of which it is written: 'He who perseveres to the end shall be saved' [Matt. 10:22, 24:13], which cannot be obtained from anyone except from him who is able to make him who stands to stand [Rom. 14:4].''

[38] Aquinas says it always saves a person because of the kind of grace it is; Molina says it always saves a person because God gives it only to those who he knows will choose to respond to it. But the effect is the same: The gift of final perseverance always works.

[39] That many Calvinist theologians are not aware of this shows a serious lack of scholarship. For example, in his book *Chosen by God* (Wheaton, Illinois: Tyndale, 1994), Presbyterian theologian R. C. Sproul attempts to redefine Calvinism as "the Augustinian view." While Calvin's view of predestination might be a variation of Augustine's view, the two are not the same. Augustine did not share Calvin's understanding of "the perseverance of the saints," and neither did the broadly Augustinian tradition. That understanding was new with Calvin. For an accurate historical discussion of the perseverance of the

Instead, their faith was informed by the biblical teaching that some who enter the sphere of grace go on to leave it.

If one defines a saint as one who has had his "saintification" completed, a Catholic can say he believes in "perseverance of the saints" (all and only the people predestined to be saints will persevere). But because of the historic associations of the phrase, it is advisable to make some change in it to avoid confusing the Thomist and Calvinist understandings of perseverance. Since in Catholic theology those who will persevere are called "the predestined," or "the elect," one might replace "perseverance of the saints" with "perseverance of the predestined" or—better—with "perseverance of the elect."

## A Thomistic TULIP

In view of all this, we propose a Thomist version of TULIP:

T = Total inability (to please God without special grace)
U = Unconditional election
L = Limited intent (for the atonement's efficacy)
I = Intrinsically efficacious grace (for salvation)
P = Perseverance of the elect

There are other ways to construct a Thomist version of TULIP, of course, but that there is even one way demonstrates that a Calvinist would not have to repudiate his understanding of predestination and grace to become Catholic. He simply would have to do

---

saints, see John Jefferson Davis' article "Perseverance of the Saints: A History of the Doctrine" in *The Journal of the Evangelical Theological Society*, 34:2[June 1991]:213–228. Davis is himself a Calvinist, but he admits that Calvin introduced the idea that one cannot lose salvation.

greater justice to the teaching of Scripture on certain points and refine his understanding of perseverance.[40]

---

[40] This has important applications for Calvinists who are thinking about entering the Church, as well as implications for Catholics who want to know what the Church requires them to believe and how they might defend the Church against anti-Catholic Calvinists. For an example of how Thomism can be used to refute Calvinist attacks on the Mass, purgatory, and indulgences, see my article "Fatally Flawed Thinking" (*This Rock*, July 1993). The article critiques *The Fatal Flaw*, a book by James White, a Calvinist and an anti-Catholic. For further reading on Catholic teaching in this area, see *Predestination* by Reginald Garrigou-Lagrange (St. Louis: Herder, 1939).

# 7

# Resisting and Cooperating with God

Many Calvinists are horrified when they hear of Catholics talking about resisting grace or cooperating with God. However, the Bible uses this language and Calvinists cannot criticize it without criticizing the language of Scripture itself.

## The Language of Resistance

With regard to resisting God, we read Stephen's excoriation of many Jewish people in his day: "You stiff-necked people, uncircumcised in heart and ears, you always resist the Holy Spirit. As your fathers did, so do you" (Acts 7:51). This language is abrasive to Calvinists; it runs against the grain of their theology because they have historically labeled a major plank of their view "irresistible grace." This was a mistake because it fossilized in Calvinist vocabulary a rejection of the simplest way to express an important biblical theme: that we must not resist the motions of the Holy Spirit, as those addressed in Acts 7:51 did.

The thing Calvinists are concerned about, the concept that there is *a* motion of God's grace that is infallibly fruitful in bringing about the repentance and salvation of a sinner, is a fine enough concept. Many Catholics, such as Thomists (and also Augustinians), believe it, too. In keeping with the language of Scripture, however, Catholics do not refer to this as "irresistible grace" but, in the case of Thomists, as "intrinsically efficacious grace"—grace that by its nature brings about its effect.

That not all grace is of this sort is indicated by the fact that the

Holy Spirit gives motions of grace that can be resisted. So in addition to intrinsically efficacious grace, Thomists say that there are also extrinsically efficacious graces, which would have to be supplemented by something else in order to produce their intended effect. Of course, the supplement would itself be a grace God has given, so in the end everything must be attributed to God's grace. This, however, does not change the point that *not* every individual grace God gives is intrinsically efficacious. Some individual graces he gives would have to be paired with other graces in order to bring about the goal, such as the grace of being able freely to cooperate with God.

Thus, for example, the Jews addressed in Acts 7 received one grace, the motions of the Holy Spirit; but from the Thomist perspective, they did not receive the grace of cooperating with those motions. A Thomist might say they were people who received partial graces but not full graces.

Calvinists use this very fact as a defensive move to explain passages such as Hebrews 6:4–6, which speaks of people "who have once been enlightened, who have tasted the heavenly gift, and have become partakers of the Holy Spirit, and have tasted the goodness of the word of God and the powers of the age to come, and have fallen away" (literal translation). Calvinists argue that these people were never real Christians. They experienced some salvation-related graces but never salvation itself. Unfortunately, this maneuver won't work because it flatly contradicts the text, but it does reveal a point of agreement between Catholics and Calvinists—that there are people who receive some salvation-related graces from the Holy Spirit that do not of themselves bring those people to full and final salvation.

The problem is that Calvinists have not integrated this into their language, so they continue to use such unbiblical modes of speech as "God's grace is irresistible," and to shudder when they hear people using such biblical modes of speech as "You always resist the Holy Spirit." Fortunately, as we saw in the last chapter, some Calvinists are trying to change the language of "irresistible grace."

## The Language of Cooperation

Related to this is the issue of the biblical language of cooperation with God, because if one does not resist God and his grace then one sometimes cooperates with God and his grace. Calvinists also sometimes become upset when Catholics talk about cooperating with God, which they denounce as the evil doctrine of "synergism" (from the Greek, "work with"). To claim that people work with God can sound blasphemous to many Calvinist ears, which is ironic because the New Testament several times uses the very term *synergize* with respect to God's action and ours. The Bible is a synergist book because in the most literal sense possible it uses synergist language. One cannot denounce the language of synergism without denouncing the language of the Bible. For example, in Mark 16:20 we read: "And they went forth and preached everywhere, while the Lord *worked with* [*sunergountos*] them and confirmed the message by the signs that attended it. Amen."

Here we have a declaration that God worked with the apostles in their ministry of preaching. This of itself shows that the language of *men cooperating* with God cannot be considered unbiblical. Indeed, the example goes beyond that and shows us that the language that speaks of *God himself* cooperating with men—speaking of *them* as the principal actors—is not unbiblical, and if the former were thought offensive by some Calvinists, the latter should be totally outrageous. What is more, we have here not just a statement that God cooperates with men in producing some natural thing, such as crops or money; we have a statement that God cooperates with men in producing salvation, since that is the goal (and result) of the apostles' preaching mission.

And this is not the only time Scripture uses *sunergeo* to refer to human-divine cooperation. In Romans 8:28 we also read that "in everything God *works for good with* [*sunergei eis agathon*] those who love him, who are called according to his purpose."[1]

---

[1] This is the reading of the best manuscripts. The old King James Version

Here we have another declaration of God working with men. As Protestant theologian Dale Moody puts it,

> God works with those who love him toward the goal of the good. [Calvinist theologian John] Murray insists that this is all "divine monergism," but the Greek verb is *sunergei*, from which the idea of a synergism between the will of God and the will of man comes. The . . . Calvinistic tradition will insert its ideas even if the very word of the text must be rejected![2]

And elsewhere Moody writes:

> The best translation of Romans 8:28 that we have noted . . . says God "cooperates for good with those who love God and are called according to his purpose." This is just right, the way the Greek reads, but this understanding has been denounced as synergism. The Greek word for "work with" is *sunergei*, and from this word synergism was formed. It is strange indeed to hear people declaring they believe in the verbal inspiration of Holy Scripture, yet at the same time they denounce this verb! They seem to find an increase in zeal as they butt their heads in an obstinate way against the very language of the Bible. What really do they mean when they speak of the inspiration and authority of Scripture, if the words of the Bible are forbidden? [*The Word of Truth*, 342].

Paul goes beyond what he says in Romans 8:28 in a verse that would make a Calvinist even more uncomfortable: "*Working together with* [*sunergountes*] him, then, we entreat you not to accept the grace of God in vain" (2 Cor. 6:1).

Here we have not only the language of men working with God (as opposed to God working with men), but Paul adds his exhortation not to accept the grace of God in vain, which indicates that the grace of God *can* be accepted in vain.

A full exegesis of this verse would have to show what grace is being talked about—whether it is the offer or the reality of salvation. But no matter what the answer to that question is, this verse

---

rendering of this verse, which suggests that all things conspire for good by a kind of automatic providence, is based on an erroneous manuscript tradition.

[2] *Broadman Bible Commentary: Romans* (Nashville: Broadman, 1970), 221.

says something incongruent with standard Calvinist language, because it means it is either possible to accept the grace of salvation at one time and then have it be vain, or it means that it is
possible to accept the grace of the offer of salvation and have it
be vain because you fail to cooperate with the offer—either of
which means that this grace is not irresistible.

Calvinists have long differentiated between God's internal and
external call to salvation. The latter is thought to be given every
time an unsaved person hears the gospel preached. The former is
thought to be given when an unsaved person not only hears the
gospel preached but also is given the grace that will cause him to
respond and accept salvation. Calvinists make use of this distinction to keep from talking about God's grace (i.e., the internal call)
being resistible and thus potentially "failing," "being frustrated,"
or "made vain," but the point is that even if this verse did refer
to the external call of God, it would still show that *some* of God's
graces can be accepted but then made vain, for the external call
is itself a grace.

Also, whichever grace it is—God's outer call, God's inner call,
or God's gift of salvation itself—it is a salvation-related grace,
meaning again that salvation-related graces, and specifically graces
that *lead toward* salvation can be resisted. It also means (and this is
especially clear if it is God's external call[3]) that in biblical language

---

[3] Although I am here speaking of the grace (to which Paul is referring)
as God's external call, this is for the Calvinist's benefit, as it is the reading
he would most likely give the text. Actually, I think that once a person gets
over the idea that a true Christian can never lose salvation, the more natural
reading of the text is that Paul is calling true Christians to remain in salvation
or calling true but fallen Christians to come back to salvation so they will
not have received the grace of God (i.e., their initial salvation) in vain (i.e.,
by dying without it).

This is indicated by the fact that Paul is talking to Christians, and, as always, presumes that unless there is evidence otherwise, all Christians are true
Christians who were genuinely converted and genuinely received salvation,
though they may have since fallen. If Paul means the grace to which he refers
to be the external call of God, that would make the passage very odd, since
his audience in the Corinthian church had already received the external call

men cooperate with God in *bestowing* salvation-related graces—another shocking mode of expression to many Calvinists.

And as Paul indicates, cooperation in bestowing the grace must be met with cooperation on the part of the person receiving the grace. Otherwise (if no action is taken) it will be rendered vain. Thus in biblical language, human cooperation is needed both in giving and in receiving this grace.

Of course, a Calvinist can say that both cooperations in the giving and the embracing of the eternal call are themselves *produced* (not just enabled) by God's grace; a Thomistic Catholic would say the same. This is perfectly acceptable from a Catholic point of view. A Calvinist and a Thomistic Catholic alike can say that our cooperation is produced by God's operation. The point is that we cannot criticize as unbiblical the language of cooperating with God in salvific matters, which is precisely what the Calvinist does.

Besides using the verb *synergize* (*sunergeo*, the verb used in different forms in the three preceding verses), Paul even uses the potentially more shocking term *synergist* (*sunergos*), "co-laborer" or "fellow worker," with respect to himself and God, saying, "For we are God's *fellow workers* [*sunergoi*]; you are God's field, God's building" (1 Cor. 3:9).

Here Paul again speaks of himself (and, by extension, other ministers of Christ) as synergists, or cooperators, with God in salvific matters, bringing the count to two verses speaking of God cooperating with men and two verses speaking of men cooperating with God.

The language of resisting or cooperating with God is simply not the theological bogeyman that many Calvinists make it out to be. In decrying it and looking down upon those who use this biblical mode of speech, such Calvinists inadvertently take a holier-than-thou attitude with respect to the language of Scripture, which, since it is God's language, means that they have inadvertently taken a holier-than-Thou attitude.

---

of God in evangelism and thus does not need an evangelistic appeal. Paul is not doing primary evangelism with them. He is not calling them *to* salvation but *back to* salvation if they have forsaken it.

# 8

# Faith, Works, and Boasting

Among the most controversial subjects in the study of salvation are the meanings of certain key words: *works, good works, works of the Law, faith,* and *boasting.* Especially controversial are the ways several of these terms are used in the New Testament by Paul and James, and how their differing modes of expression can be harmonized.

We need to begin by stepping back and looking at how these terms are used in Scripture. "Works of the Law" would be better translated as "works of Torah" to facilitate people's understanding of what Paul is talking about. The phrase in Greek, *erga nomou,* is usually translated as "works of the Law"—"law" being the standard translation of the Greek word *nomos.* However, *nomos* was the word that the Greek Old Testament—the Septuagint—used to translate the Hebrew word *Torah,* which doesn't quite mean *law* (some have suggested *instruction* or *teaching* would be better English equivalents). In any event, when Paul speaks of "works of the Law," the context makes it clear that the law he has in mind is the Torah, or Law of Moses, as found in the first five books of the Bible (Genesis through Deuteronomy).

This makes it better to translate *erga nomou* as "works of Torah." If one doesn't use the specific word *Torah,* English speakers tend to lose track of what law Paul is talking about, since for them the mere word *law* does not invariably conjure the mental impression of the Mosaic Law, as it did for a first-century Jew, such as Paul.

The translation of *erga nomou* as "works of Torah" is supported by archaeological-lexical evidence. The phrase also appears in Hebrew in the Dead Sea Scrolls, the writings of the first-century

Qumran community in Israel. It appears in a famous document known as *Miqsat Ma'ase ha-Torah* (or 4QMMT, or simply MMT), which served essentially as the declaration of independence for the Qumran community. This document, whose name translates as "Some Works of Torah," focuses on certain disputed interpretations of specific Mosaic regulations and states that it is the violation of these regulations that led the Qumran sect to separate itself from worship at the Jerusalem Temple—because the priests there weren't doing the works of Torah properly. It also seeks to persuade the individual to whom it is addressed to adopt the sect's views.

MMT reveals a preoccupation on the part of many first-century Jews with works of Torah, and it sheds great light on the meaning of the term in Paul.[1] The important thing for us to note is that the term "works of Torah" predates Paul. He picked it up from the Jewish vocabulary of his day, which is why there is a dispute regarding it in Romans and Galatians—because his opponents are already using the term.

The first occurrence of the phrase in Paul is in Romans 3:20. Before this point in Romans, the term *ergon* ("work" or "deed") and its cognates were found only in Romans 2:6, 7, and 15. In none of these places does the term indicate what Paul has in mind in 3:20.

In 2:6, Paul states that God will judge every man according to his works. Obviously he does not mean works of Torah because the judgment of Gentiles was in view as well as the judgment of Jews (cf. 2:9–10).

In 2:7 Paul says that God will reward those who persevered "in well-doing" (literally, "good work") by giving them eternal life, or immortality (as well as glory and honor). But this is precisely what Paul says works of Torah will *not* get one because Torah does

---

[1] See the three articles related to the subject in the Nov./Dec. 1994 issue of *Biblical Archaeology Review* and R. Eisenman's and M. Wise's book *The Dead Sea Scrolls Uncovered* (New York: Penguin, 1993), ch. 6, "Works Reckoned as Righteousness—Legal Texts."

not give the power to deal with sin. Thus there is a distinction in Paul's mind between "good work(s)" and "works of Torah."

In 2:15 Paul states that when Gentiles do by nature what Torah requires, they show that "what the Torah requires" (literally, "the work [singular] of Torah") is written on their hearts. This is the core of Torah—the important part, which God has written on the hearts even of Gentiles. It is the same thing Paul has in mind in 8:4 when he says that God has done what Torah could not do by sending his Son "in order that the just [righteous] requirement of the Torah might be fulfilled in us." "The work of Torah" in 2:15 is the same as "the righteous requirement of the Torah" in 8:4. It, not all the Torah's commands about diet and festival and ceremony, is what is written on the hearts of Gentiles, and it is what Paul says in 8:4 that God sent his Son to empower us to accomplish.

Thus the introduction of the term "works [plural] of Torah" in 3:20 is a new theme in the epistle, separate from the general "works" (actions, whether good or bad) according to which men will be judged, separate from the "good work" that God will reward with eternal life, and separate from the "work [singular] of the Law" that is written on the hearts of Gentiles and which Christ came to enable us to fulfill. Because of its distinction from these things, we must inquire more closely into what Paul means by the term. Unfortunately, the context here does not give us much of a clue, but the concept becomes clear as we proceed. Once the term "works of Torah" has been introduced, evidence accumulates rapidly concerning what Paul has in mind.

In 3:28, Paul reiterates his thesis that "a man is justified by faith apart from works of Torah."[2] To support this, he asks rhetorically, "Or is God the God of Jews only? Is he not the God of Gentiles also? Yes, of Gentiles also" (3:29). "Works of Torah" must therefore be characteristic of Jews rather than Gentiles. This

---

[2] In biblical quotations containing the phrase "works of Torah," unless otherwise noted the translation we use will continue to be the RSV:CE but with the word "Torah" replacing "law."

supports the identification of the Law that Paul is talking about as the Torah, since this was the only law characteristic of Jews but not Gentiles.

It is in chapter 4 that we have the first *concrete* example of what Paul means by "works of Torah," and the example, confirming what we have just seen, is circumcision (4:9–12). Paul emphasizes with great force the nonnecessity of circumcision for justification. In fact, the whole purpose of his discussion, in chapter 4, of Abraham as the father of the faithful is to show the nonnecessity of circumcision for being right with God.

Paul was concerned with circumcision in particular because it was the Jewish rite of initiation, just as baptism is for Christians. By being baptized one becomes part of the New Covenant and a member of the Christian people; by being circumcised one becomes part of the Mosaic Covenant and a member of the Jewish people. Many at the time thought that one could not be saved without becoming a Jew, and it is this idea that Paul is concerned to stop.

Because circumcision was the Jewish rite of initiation, which makes one part of the Mosaic Covenant, Paul views circumcision as the work of Torah par excellence—something reflected earlier in the epistle, when he conducted an extended discussion of the irrelevance of circumcision to salvation (2:25–3:1), and when, right after his affirmation in 3:27 that works of Torah are not necessary, he drew the inference that God "will justify the circumcised on the ground of their faith and the uncircumcised through their faith" (3:30). The identification of "works of Law" with "works of Torah" is thus confirmed by the discussion of circumcision in Romans.

It is further confirmed by the discussion of circumcision in Galatians. There, Paul greatly stresses the fact that Titus was not compelled to be circumcised at Jerusalem (Gal. 2:3). Paul characterizes the agitators who prompted Peter to behave hypocritically as "the circumcision party" (Gal. 2:12). He emphasizes that "if you receive circumcision, Christ will profit you nothing" (Gal. 5:2). His statement that "every man who receives circumcision

. . . is bound to keep the whole Torah" (Gal. 5:3) indicates that circumcision, which was at the forefront of the debate over Torah, was the sign of embracing Torah as a whole. And he states that "in Christ Jesus neither circumcision nor uncircumcision is of any avail" (Gal. 5:6).

Paul emphasizes the difference between his preaching and the preaching of circumcision by asking, "But if I . . . still preach circumcision, why am I still persecuted?" (Gal. 5:11). He goes on to state that he wishes the circumcisers "would go the whole way and emasculate themselves!" (Gal. 5:12, NIV). He warns his readers that those "that would compel you to be circumcised . . . [do so] only in order that they may not be persecuted" (Gal. 6:12). "Even those who receive circumcision," he adds, "do not themselves keep the Torah, but they desire to have you circumcised that they may glory in your flesh" (Gal. 6:13). Finally, he reminds his readers again that "neither circumcision counts for anything, nor uncircumcision, but a new creation" (Gal. 6:15).

But while circumcision is the work of Torah par excellence, Paul has in mind that there are other works of Torah, as indicated by the text of Galatians. When Paul reminds Peter in Galatians 2:16 that they both "know that a man is not justified by works of Torah," it is in a context in which Peter and the other Jewish Christians had separated themselves from eating with the Gentile Christians of Antioch (Gal. 2:12–13). This was because Gentiles were regarded as unclean and ate unclean food (cf. Acts 10:9–16 with 11:3–12). Eating with Gentiles thus indicated a breach of the separation between clean and unclean people (clearly stressed in the Torah) and a partaking of unclean food (also stressed in the Torah). Thus the laws of separation between clean and unclean are in view when Paul discusses "works of Torah."

Paul also laments that the Galatians "observe [Jewish ceremonial] days, and months, and seasons, and years!" (Gal. 4:10). This indicates that, in addition to circumcision, separation laws, and food laws, Jewish festival laws are also subsumed under what Paul has in mind when he speaks of "works of Torah."

Many have noted that when Paul speaks of the works of Torah, he gives examples that later interpreters would say pertain to the ceremonial precepts of the Mosaic Law.[3] But a question arises concerning whether Paul has in mind *only* the ceremonial works of Torah when he uses the phrase. Does he also have in mind the moral "work of Torah" that is written on the hearts of Gentiles? Many Protestant preachers assume that he does, but this is a judgment that would have to be established by exegesis rather than by assertion.

Since Torah in Paul's thought was a united whole, not a composite of two or three distinct codes—moral, ceremonial, judicial —someone might suppose that when Paul says works of Torah are irrelevant to salvation, he means nothing in Torah is necessary, whether ceremonial or moral. But this is a faulty inference. Arguing that a united whole is unnecessary does not mean that all of its elements are unnecessary. To assert that it does mean this is to commit what is known in logic as the fallacy of division (i.e., the whole has a certain property—nonnecessity, in this case—therefore each of the parts has this property as well). A dietitian might tell us that drinking Diet Coke is not necessary to good health, but we would not at all be permitted to draw the inference from this that drinking water (the principal ingredient of Diet Coke) is not necessary to good health. In the same way, we cannot simply assume from the fact that Torah is not necessary

---

[3] The phrase "ceremonial works of Torah" is to be preferred to the phrase "works of the ceremonial Law," since Paul does not speak of a ceremonial Torah in contrast to a moral Torah or a judicial (or civil) Torah. The tripartite division of Torah into moral, judicial (or civil), and ceremonial commands, while a useful division at times, is an anachronism not found in Paul's thought. The precepts of the Torah *can* be classified according to those three categories, but Paul does not himself make that division. If any division were at the fore of Paul's mind, it would be between things Torah mentions that Christians do have to do and things Torah mentions that Christians do not have to do. But even then he does not speak of two separate Torahs but of one Torah—which mentions some things that are obligatory for Christians and some things that are not. (We will see later *why* the ones that are obligatory for Christians are binding; it *isn't* because the Torah mentions them.)

to salvation that none of the things in the Torah are necessary to salvation. This is abundantly shown by the fact that one of the things commanded in the Torah is belief in God, which on anyone's account *is* necessary for salvation.[4]

Because of these considerations, one cannot argue from Paul's view of a united Torah to the conclusion that he is saying that every element of Torah is unnecessary. Indeed, at least one element of Torah—belief in God—is necessary. That particular item mandated in Torah *is* required.

Yet because of the united nature of Torah in Paul's mind, we cannot understand the unnecessary "works of Torah" to mean only certain no-longer-necessary aspects of Torah, such as its ceremonial precepts. Instead, "works of Torah" means any act—whether moral, ceremonial, or judicial—that is undertaken to fulfill the requirements of the Law of Moses. In other words, if someone is doing things because they are prescribed in Torah, then that person is doing works of Torah.

This leaves open the question of *why* a person is doing works of Torah. Is it because he wishes to live as a Jew and does it as a matter of Jewish custom only? Is it because he is a Jewish Christian who feels that—as a Jew—he is obligated to do it, even though Gentile Christians are not? Or is it because he feels that salvation itself hinges on willingness to live under Torah?

Let's consider the first of these options. What would Paul say about someone who does works of Torah for cultural rather than theological reasons? Paul is not opposed to people who were born Jewish continuing their ancestral customs, at least for the time being.[5] He is not concerned with and never condemns people for doing works of Torah because they are Jews and are simply observing Jewish custom. At least in the transitional era in which he lived, Paul doesn't think that Christian Jews have to cease attend-

---

[4] Even if it is implicit faith.

[5] A case could be made that Paul would acknowledge the coming of a post-Temple, post-synagogue age in which Jewish Christians should not continue certain rites.

ing the synagogue or the Temple or similar things. This is his point when he said, "Was any one at the time of his call [to Christ] already circumcised? Let him not seek to remove the marks of circumcision. Was any one at the time of his call uncircumcised? Let him not seek circumcision" (1 Cor. 7:18).

Paul even was not opposed to administering circumcision to individuals as long as it was understood that this was not being done to obtain salvation. We read in Acts 16:

> Paul wanted Timothy to accompany him; and he took him and circumcised him because of the Jews that were in those places, for they all knew that his father was a Greek. As they went on their way through the cities, they delivered to them for observance the decisions which had been reached by the apostles and elders who were at Jerusalem [Acts 16:3–4].

Here Paul circumcises Timothy, whose mother was Jewish, to enable him to minister better to the Jewish people he would encounter on the missionary journey they were pursuing. Timothy thus accepted circumcision by Paul as an act of adherence to Jewish *culture*, not for salvation. We know that it was already very clear in Paul's mind that circumcision was not needed for salvation because this is *after* the Acts 15 council which decreed that Gentiles did not need to be circumcised.

That had been a great victory for Paul, who had been preaching it for a long time, and it was these very "decisions which had been reached by the apostles and elders who were at Jerusalem" that he was anxious to deliver to the churches in the cities on their journey. Yet in the midst of his "circumcision is unnecessary" triumph, Paul circumcises Timothy! We can only conclude from this, and from his exhortation to Jews not to seek to be uncircumcised that Paul does not object to circumcision and other works of Torah as long as they are being done as matters of custom and not as paths to salvation.

What of the second option we mentioned—the case of a Jewish Christian performing works of Torah because he believes that he is obligated as a Jew to do them, though Gentile Christians are not?

Ultimately, Paul would say that Jewish Christians are not bound to do works of Torah, for he tells us that Christ "abolish[ed] in his flesh the Torah of commandments and ordinances" (Eph. 2:15) and that he himself was not under Torah (1 Cor. 9:20).

However, for the sake of ecclesiastical peace and for the sake of individuals' consciences, he seems content to allow Jewish Christians to continue to act on the premise that they are still obligated by Torah. Thus he acknowledges that all foods are lawful and that one is not bound to observe Jewish holy days, but he allows a conscience exception for those who feel differently (Rom. 14). He only objects to people doing works of Torah when they cause harm—such as making Gentile Christians feel like second-class citizens (as was the case in Antioch; Gal. 2:11–16)—or when they are used as a repudiation of the Christian faith (as the author of Hebrews is concerned with) or when people have the idea that salvation is tied to them.

This leads us to the third reason someone might be doing works of Torah. Paul is very concerned when individuals begin saying —as happened at Antioch, Rome, and Galatia—that "unless you are circumcised according to the custom of Moses, you cannot be saved" (Acts 15:1). That presents the Mosaic Law, rather than Jesus Christ, as the basis of salvation, and that constitutes a false gospel (Gal. 1:8–9). It is at this point that customs such as circumcision and keeping kosher become a problem. As long as they are not done to achieve salvation, they are permissible for Paul. But when they are done as requirements for salvation, a false gospel is being pursued.

To understand Paul's thought on this subject better, we need to consider another aspect of what he teaches. At the same time that Paul is emphatic that works of Torah are not necessary, he also *exhorts* people to do good works—including many good works taught in the Torah itself, such as love of God and love of neighbor, the two great commandments of the Torah (Matt. 22:36–40, 2 Thess. 3:5, cf. Rom. 13:9). He thus excoriates reliance on works of Torah for salvation, but commands certain things Torah enumerates—things (such as faith) that *are* required for salvation. How are we to understand this paradox?

Part of the explanation is that Paul is free to exhort people to do good things—have faith, love God, love one's neighbor—as long as the individual doesn't get the idea that he must obey the Torah generally to be saved. The real question is: If we're not obliged to obey the Torah in general, why are these particular things required of us? The answer is: Because there is something else—something other than the Torah—that requires them of us. They may be *mentioned* in the Torah, but *that* isn't what obligates us to do them.

The real reason that we must do these things is that they are commanded by a higher law that is reflected both in the Torah and in the hearts of men (Rom. 2:15), and in a law that unambiguously applies to Christians—the Law of Christ (1 Cor. 9:21, Gal. 6:2). To understand this, one needs to understand the relationships among the different forms of divine law.

The most basic and fundamental law is known in theology as the eternal law. It consists of God's wisdom, his plan for the universe, by which all creation is directed. One subset of the eternal law is known as the natural law. In the sciences this term has a different meaning, but in theology the natural law is understood to be rational creatures' participation in the eternal law—namely, those things that reason tells us about God's plan and how we as rational creatures ought to behave (e.g., that murder, lying, and stealing are wrong). It is this law which Paul tells us that God has written in the hearts of men (Rom. 2:15), whether they be Jew or Gentile. Unfortunately, due to the effects of sin, our perception of this law is often faulty (Rom. 1:19–28), therefore, to keep us from rationalizing sin, it helps to have an explicit statement of what God requires.

This need has led God to give two bodies of what is called positive law. Positive law, in this context, consists of law that is communicated to man overtly, by divine revelation.[6] The two bodies of positive law that God has given are known in theology as the

---

[6] There is also such a thing as human positive law—laws decreed by human government—but here we are concerned with divine positive law—i.e., laws proclaimed by God in special revelation.

Old Law and the New Law and known in the Bible as the Law of Moses (i.e., the Torah) and the Law of Christ. Both of these bodies of law contain material found in the natural law (and thus in the eternal law), such as that one should love God and love one's neighbor. They also both contain particular positive precepts (i.e., explicitly stated precepts) that apply only to the ages in which the laws are in operation (and thus are not part of eternal law, since the latter is immutable). For example, the Law of Moses commands circumcision, the observance of the Sabbath, and the creation of cities of refuge within Israel (Ex. 20:8–11, Num. 35:2). The Law of Christ commands baptism, the reception of the Eucharist, and the observance of the Lord's Day (Matt. 28:19, John 6:53–54, 1 Cor. 16:2, Rev. 1:10).

Thus the reason we Christians are obligated to obey the Ten Commandments is not that they are commanded by the Law of Moses. We as Christians are not obligated to obey the Law of Moses. In fact, the only people who were *ever* bound to obey the Law of Moses were the Jewish people prior to the time of Christ (ST I-II:98:5). Christians are, however, bound to obey the natural law that God has written in their hearts and the Law of Christ (1 Cor. 9:21). This is explained in the section on the Third Commandment in the *Roman Catechism*:[7]

> The other Commandments of the Decalogue [except the third, or Sabbath command] are precepts of the natural law, obligatory at all times and unalterable. Hence, after the abrogation of the Law of Moses . . . the Commandments contained in the two tables are observed by Christians, not indeed because their observance is commanded by Moses, but because they are in conformity with nature, which dictates obedience to them.

This understanding of why Christians must keep the moral precepts found in the Law of Moses—because they are *also* found in the natural law (Rom. 1:19–20, 2:14) or in the Law of Christ (Gal. 6:2)—resolves the paradox in Paul's writings of praising good

---

[7] Also known as the *Catechism of the Council of Trent*; not the same as the *Catechism of the Catholic Church*.

works, including ones named in the Law of Moses, but condemning reliance on works of Torah (Gal. 3:10).

It also explains why he insists that Christians do certain things named in the Torah (i.e., have faith, love God, love neighbor), but insists that other things (circumcision, kosher diet, Jewish feasts) are irrelevant to salvation (Gal. 5:6) or even harmful to it (Gal. 5:2). The rule is: Only the moral precepts of the Torah that are found in the natural law and therefore in the Law of Christ, which makes them binding on us (though even then they are not binding *because* the Torah mentions them). The commands of Torah that are ceremonial or judicial in nature are not binding on us except insofar as they contain a moral element. If ceremonial or judicial works of Torah are done as a matter of ethnic custom (as with Timothy), they are harmless. If they are done to achieve salvation, they are harmful—indeed, deadly—because they are being observed in pursuit of a false gospel.

Fundamental in Paul's mind is a separation between two different systems of salvation: one in which a person seeks to be put right with God through the Torah and one in which a person seeks to be put right with God through Jesus Christ. This contrast between the system of salvation by Torah and salvation by Christ is the key to understanding one aspect of the letter to the Romans that is otherwise very difficult to grasp, namely, Paul's discussion of Jewish and Christian boasting.

## Jewish Boasting in Romans

A theme in Romans that deserves special mention is boasting of one's relationship to God. This is something Paul speaks of both Jews and Christians doing. He speaks of Jews boasting a number of times:

> You call yourself a Jew and rely upon the Torah and boast of your relation to God [2:17, literally, "in God"].

> You who boast in Torah, do you dishonor God by breaking Torah? [2:23].

> Then what becomes of our boasting? It is excluded. On what principle? On the principle of works? No, but on the principle of faith [3:27].

> For if Abraham was justified by works, he has something to boast about, but not before God [4:2].

Many Protestants take the passages in Romans that speak of Jews boasting and use them to argue that they describe a self-righteousness and an attempt to earn one's place before God by one's own efforts. It is claimed that in these passages the people in question were boasting about their own righteous deeds. As we will see, this is a misrepresentation of the text.

While in contemporary English usage the idea of boasting normally connotes arrogance, this is not always the case in Greek. The word used by Paul—*kauchaomai*—means not just to boast but also to glory, to rejoice, and to exult. The point is: It's not automatically negative, the way the word "boast" is in English. Indeed, we will see later that Paul *recommends* "boasting" about certain things. So one must not assume that he's criticizing people for "boasting" in the English sense. One should take the term in a neutral fashion until there is evidence that it is to be taken otherwise.[8]

Now, let's look at what Paul says the Jewish person is boasting in. Is it his own moral deeds? No. In Romans 2:17 Paul says the Jewish person is boasting "in God," talking about how great God is. He is, as Jeremiah put it, "glorying in the Lord" (Jer. 9:24). Here the object of the Jew's boast is God—Yahweh—not his own self-righteous works. He is boasting to the Gentile, saying, "*My* God is greater than *your* god," not boasting in front of the Lord saying, "Look how righteous *I* am, God."

Similarly, in Romans 2:23 we see that the object of the Jew's boasting is the Torah. Paul addresses those "who boast in Torah."

---

[8] See 1 Cor. 9:15, 15:31; 2 Cor. 2:12, 14, 7:4, 14, 8:24, 9:2–4, 10:8, 13–16, 11:10; 2 Thess. 1:4. See also 2 Cor. 10:16–17; Rom. 15:17; 1 Cor. 1:31, 3:21; 2 Cor. 5:12.

Here again the object of the boast is not the Jewish person's own righteous performance but the Torah *itself*. The Torah is an object of boasting in front of Gentiles because it is seen as a divine gift. The Jew thus reasons in front of his Gentile neighbor: "How glorious is Torah! It is the wisdom of God and his gift to his people!"

That the Jew is not boasting about his own moral accomplishments is evident because, immediately after acknowledging the Jewish person's boast in the Torah, Paul asks, "Do you dishonor God by breaking Torah? For, as it is written, 'The name of God is blasphemed among the Gentiles because of you'" (3:23–24). Paul pricks his reader's conscience by pointing out that the Jewish person himself has broken Torah. He says, in effect, "Okay, so you glorify God's Torah in front of Gentiles. But do you dishonor God in front of Gentiles by breaking his Torah?"

Of course, Paul does not deny that the greatness of the first five books of the Bible should be celebrated. But he is concerned with the idea of many Jewish people in the first century that if one wanted to follow God then one was obligated to become a Jew and embrace the Torah. The Torah had, in many circles, come to be seen as *the* way to be united with God. The Gentiles do not keep Torah, it was reasoned, so they are not united to God. For Jews who had this idea, their boasting in God and in the Torah was problematic. Nowhere in the Torah or anywhere else in the Old Testament did God say that one had to become a Jew to be saved. As the revelation of the Christian age made clear, this first-century idea was false.

But at the time, many Jewish Christians were preaching it. They boasted before Gentiles of the greatness of God and the greatness of the Torah as necessary for being united to God, so that only Jews could be saved. This is not boasting of self-righteous accomplishments. The focus is still on the Torah and the Mosaic Covenant as a *gift* from God, as a *grace* given to his chosen people. Jewish people recognized that their relationship with God was one of grace and loving-kindness, as many contemporary Protestant commentators have noted (including E. P. Sanders and James D. G. Dunn). Paul knows this, and he is not criticizing his opponents because he thinks they are trying to earn their position before God. What he has a problem with is their claim that everyone who wants to be saved has to become a Jew.

This form of boasting is not without an element of pride—pride not in one's own moral accomplishments, but in one's favored position with God. We see this in Romans 2:17–21:

> But if you call yourself a Jew and rely upon Torah and boast [in God] and know his will and approve what is excellent, because you are instructed in Torah, and if you are sure that you are a guide to the blind, a light to those who are in darkness, a corrector of the foolish, a teacher of children, having in Torah the embodiment of knowledge and truth—you then who teach others, will you not teach yourself? [Rom. 2:17–21].

The self-image Paul paints for his opponents is indeed one involving pride, but the focus is not on their righteous acts but on the blessing they believe themselves to have because of Torah.

Some modern readers, however, may have difficulty understanding the difference between pridefully boasting about one's accomplishments and pridefully boasting about one's relationship to God, so an analogy may be helpful. Imagine two boys bickering, one adopting a superior attitude and saying, "Well, *my* dad is better than *your* dad." In this case, the child is boasting about his father and his relationship with his father, not about anything he has done himself. This is not unlike a Jew pridefully saying before a Gentile, "*My* God is better than *your* god. I have the living God, and you have only dead idols."

Now let's change the analogy a little to bring out the favored relationship aspect. Suppose there are two children in a family, one born to the mother and father, the other adopted. The natural child may say to the adopted child, "Well *I* was born to Mom and Dad, *not* adopted; I'm their *real* child." In this case he is boasting of having a relationship to the parents that is superior to that of the other child. The argument is that because the one child lacks a certain quality (being a natural child), he must therefore lack the favored relationship of the first child. A child may even boast that he is more favored by the parents on the basis of having greater knowledge. Thus an older child may tell a younger child, "Mom and Dad like me better because *I* am in first grade, while *you* aren't even in kindergarten yet."

This is, essentially, the boast that Paul's opponents were making to Gentiles: "*We* are God's children by the *covenant* he made through Moses, and that Law of Moses gives us perfect knowledge of his will. If *you* want to be right with the living God, *you* must become part of the covenant, too, by being circumcised and living under Torah."

Living under Torah, of course, did not mean living sinlessly. Dealing with sin was the purpose of many of the rituals and sacrifices that Torah itself prescribed. Jewish people—especially in an age when the Temple was still in operation—were fully aware of this, and Paul does not imagine that his opponents believed that they had to live sinlessly in order to be acceptable to God. Indeed, no Jew would believe such a thing. It was enough, when one sinned, to repent and take the course of action prescribed by Torah for the kind of sin one had committed. *That* was life under the Covenant. Otherwise, what could the Torah mean by all of its prescriptions for dealing with sin?

So Paul is not faulting his opponents because he thinks that they are trying to earn their place before God by good works. His problem is not that they are failing to take into account the role of grace. His problem is that they think that living under Torah—including its sacrifices for sin—is the thing that puts them right with God, that it is necessary and sufficient for being put right with God. In fact, it is neither. It is not necessary, so Gentiles do not need to become Jews. And it is not sufficient, for as the letter to the Hebrews points out, the sacrifices and rituals authorized for dealing with sin are fundamentally incapable of dealing with sin's eternal consequences (Heb. 10:4). What *is* both necessary and sufficient for being put right with God is a proper relationship with Christ. *He* is the one who saves, not Torah.

Paul thus rebukes those who, as Romans 2:17 puts it, "rely upon Torah" and on that basis "boast in God." Jews do not have a saving relationship with God either on the basis of being children of Abraham (Rom. 4:11–12, 9:7; cf. Matt. 3:9) or on the basis of living under Torah. To correct this attitude, Paul stresses that "no human being will be justified in his [God's] sight by works of Torah" (Rom. 3:20) and that, instead, God "justifies him who has faith in Jesus" (3:26). In the very next verse he says, "Then what becomes of our boasting? It is excluded. On what principle? Of works? No, but on the principle of faith. For we hold that a man is justified by faith apart from works of Torah" (Rom. 3:27).

Just prior to this, Paul stated that Jews are also under the power of sin and that the Gentiles *can* be justified by faith in Jesus Christ (Rom. 3:19–26). So how must contemporary Jewish boasting before Gentiles be evaluated? It is excluded because, according to the principle of faith in Christ, those who have faith in Jesus are put right with God.[9] That being the case, Jewish boasting about having a special relationship with God through Torah is ruled out.

Notice that Paul says the principle of works *does not* exclude boasting. This has implications for the kind of boasting being considered. If it were boasting about righteousness based on one's own efforts then Paul would say that that the principle of works *does* exclude such boasting: "for even those who receive circumcision do not themselves keep the Torah" (Gal. 6:13) and Jewish people "are under the power of sin" (Rom. 3:9). If it were boasting about one's own moral purity, then Paul would say that the principle of *works* excludes boasting. But since he says the opposite, we must

---

[9] Frequently, this passage is used to argue that things such as repentance and baptism are not necessary for salvation. However, this is a misuse of the text. Paul's opponents are Jewish Christians who are telling Gentile Christians that they must become Jews. The controversy is thus taking place in a post-baptismal context and does not address the subject of how one becomes a Christian. The people Paul is trying to keep from being circumcised had already repented and been baptized. The question at hand is: For Gentile Christians, is it enough simply to continue having faith in Christ or do they need to be circumcised as well? Because the context is post-repentance, post-baptism, this text cannot be used to deny things Scripture elsewhere says about repentance and baptism (e.g., Matt. 3:7–10, 1 Pet. 3:21).

conclude that the boasting he is talking about is not boasting in self-accomplishment. Instead, it is boasting about the Jews' privileged relationship with God.

Finally, the reference to boasting in Romans 4:2 further confirms that this kind of boasting is under discussion: "What then shall we say about Abraham, our forefather according to the flesh? For if Abraham was justified by works, he has something to boast about, but not before God. For what does the Scripture say? 'Abraham believed God, and it was reckoned to him as righteousness.'"

Paul argues that Abraham was justified by faith without works. He does this by offering a common-ground principle, with which he expects his Jewish audience to agree, that "if Abraham was justified by works, he has something to boast about" (4:2). This common-ground principle would hold true regardless of how works are interpreted. If the works are acts of personal accomplishment, a person who has been justified by works would obviously have grounds on which to boast. "Look what I have done!" such a person would have a right to cry. "See, God, I have justified myself before you!" Similarly, if the works are, as we maintain, acts done to live in accord with Torah (including its prescriptions for dealing with sin), a person justified by those acts would also have grounds to boast. He could say to a Gentile: "See: I am right with God, while you are not. I have obtained his favor by living in accord with Torah."

But Paul does not stop at this point. His next comment tells us what kind of works and what kind of boasting are being talked about, for he says that a person justified by works would have grounds to boast, *"but not before God"* (4:2). If the works and boasting Paul was talking about were of personal moral accomplishment, then this last statement would make no sense. A person justified by his moral accomplishments *would* have grounds to boast in front of God. He could look to God and say, "See, Lord, all of the wonderful things I have done that have earned me my place before you."

Therefore Paul is not talking about that kind of boasting or works. That interpretation would render unintelligible his statement about not being able to boast before God. But the alternative makes perfect sense. If Abraham was justified by keeping Torah, he could boast of this before Gentiles, yet this would give him no grounds for boasting before God since Torah, with its prescriptions for dealing with sin, is itself a gift from God.

This reading not only makes the statement intelligible, but perfectly suits it for the kind of common-ground argument Paul is making. Any Jewish person hearing Paul's argument could be expected to say at this point, "Yes. That's obvious. Just because Abraham might have had grounds to boast in front of Gentiles does not mean he had grounds to boast in front of God."

A Jewish person would know that he, like any person, must adopt an attitude of humility, not boasting, before God. As the prophet says, "the LORD requires you . . . to walk humbly with your God" (Mic. 6:8). This would strike a Jewish individual as so obvious as to be axiomatic. Yet his opponents had strayed in thinking that circumcision and Torah were necessary as well. This made their boasting misplaced because—contrary to what they believed—they were not put right with God by Torah.

This suffices for an analysis of Paul's remarks on Jewish boasting. As we see in Romans 5:1-11, however, Paul has something quite different to say about Christian boasting: He recommends it.

## CHRISTIAN BOASTING IN ROMANS

While a discussion of Jewish boasting in front of unbelievers occupied Paul in Romans 2-4, in Romans 5:1-2 he takes up the parallel subject of Christian boasting in front of unbelievers: "Therefore, since we are justified by faith, let us have peace with God[10]

---

[10] Some render vv. 1-2 as saying "since we are justified by faith, *we have peace* with God," which sometimes is then used to claim that peace with God is an automatic consequence of justification that can never be lost. In most manuscripts, however, what Paul says is this: "Therefore, since we are justified by faith, *let us have peace* with God." Justification provides the basis of our relationship with God and does make our initial peace with God, but we must continue to live at peace with God and at war with sin rather than sliding back

through our Lord Jesus Christ. Through him we have obtained access to this grace in which we stand, and let us boast in our hope of sharing the glory of God."

Earlier, Paul rejected Jewish boasting in God as improper because it was based on Torah (2:23). Now he discusses Christian boasting in God, which is proper because it is based on Christ (5:11). The goal of Christian boasting in God is to win people to the Christian faith (cf. 11:13). In chapter 5 of Romans, Paul tells us to boast in three things: our hope (v. 2), our sufferings (v. 3), and God himself through Christ (v. 11).

In Romans 5:2, the term that is translated in most Bibles as "rejoice" should be "boast." It is the same word (*kauchaomai*) that already has been consistently translated as "boast" previously in Romans. Translating the term consistently makes explicit the contrast between the Jewish boasting that Paul has previously discussed and the Christian boasting he now discusses.

The first thing about which Paul says we should boast as Christians is our hope of sharing the glory of God. Contemporary preaching needs to pay attention to this statement. As part of evangelism, we should speak of our Christian hope as a way of making Christianity attractive to those who do not have this hope.

In 5:3 Paul goes beyond this and says, "More than that, let us boast in our sufferings" (literal translation). Human nature does not normally boast in sufferings, so we need to be encouraged to do so. Paul explains why in vv. 3–5: Suffering triggers a chain of events that will end up fulfilling our hope (of sharing in the glory of God; v. 2). We will not be disappointed in this hope because God's love has been poured (infused) into our hearts through the Holy Spirit (v. 5).

To illustrate the depth of God's love for us, Paul points out

---

into our sinful, pre-Christian lifestyle. Some Protestants have chosen a minority textual variant for dogmatic reasons, contrary to the manuscript evidence. Even if the minority reading were correct, however, it would in no way imply that justification cannot be lost—simply that those who are currently justified are currently at peace.

that Christ was willing to die for us when we were still sinners (that is, before we became Christians; vv. 6, 8). This goes beyond what one person will naturally do for another (v. 7), showing the supernatural character of God's love. Because of Christ's blood and death, we have been justified (v. 9) and reconciled (v. 10), so how much more will we be saved through Christ's risen life from God's wrath on the last day! Thus we should not be afraid to boast of our sufferings as Christians. We should, however, especially boast about our relationship with God through Christ. In 5:11, Paul tells us that "we also rejoice [literally, 'boast'] in God through our Lord Jesus Christ, through whom we have now received our reconciliation." This is the apex of Christian boasting.

Jewish boasting in God was misplaced because it claimed one was justified through the Torah, but Christian boasting in God is appropriate because it recognizes that it is through Christ that we have received reconciliation. Both Jewish boasting in front of unbelievers and Christian boasting in front of unbelievers are boasts "in God" rather than in one's own righteousness. Of course, we must never be arrogant when we speak of our faith, but we should make the faith attractive to others by humbly showing how great is the grace God has given us.

## The Effectiveness of Christian versus Jewish Boasting

The final reference to Christian boasting in Romans is in 15:17, where Paul tells us, "I have reason to boast in Christ Jesus in the things which pertain to God" (literal translation). The context makes clear what he is talking about:

> I have written more boldly to you on some points, as reminding you, because of the grace given to me by God, that I might be a minister of Jesus Christ to the Gentiles, ministering the gospel of God, that the offering of the Gentiles might be acceptable, sanctified by the Holy Spirit. Therefore I have reason to glory [literally, "boast"] in Christ Jesus in the things which pertain to God. For I will not dare to speak of any of those things which Christ has not accomplished through me, in word and deed, to make the Gentiles

obedient—in mighty signs and wonders, by the power of the Spirit
of God, so that from Jerusalem and round about to Illyricum I have
fully preached the gospel of Christ [Rom. 15:15–19, NKJV].

Paul, again, is not boasting of his own accomplishments. He is explicit about that: "I will not dare to speak of any of those things
which Christ has not accomplished through me." So his only
boasting of his work is boasting "in Christ Jesus in the things
which pertain to God." Rather than boasting of his righteousness in front of God, he is boasting of Christ's accomplishments
through him—"in mighty signs and wonders, by the power of the
Spirit of God." Accomplished why? "To make the Gentiles obedient" to the faith—again an evangelistic purpose to the boasting.

Earlier in Romans, he told us he does this kind of boasting a lot:
"Inasmuch then as I am an apostle to the Gentiles, I magnify my
ministry in order to make my fellow Jews jealous, and thus save
some of them" (Rom. 11:13–14). In front of his Jewish brothers,
therefore, Paul thus boasts of how many converts he has won to
Christ and to God in an attempt to make them desirous ("jealous") of having what Paul has—the Christian faith—so that they
also may be saved.

The issue of the conversion of the Gentiles was important to
Jews of the first century. The conversion of the Gentiles to God
had been repeatedly prophesied in the Old Testament, and many
first-century Jews were striving to fulfill this prophecy by preaching about ("boasting in") God in front of Gentiles. Jesus himself
notes their zeal in doing this. "Woe to you, scribes and Pharisees,
hypocrites!" he says. "You traverse sea and land to make a single
proselyte, and when he becomes a proselyte, you make him twice
as much a child of hell as yourselves!" (Matt. 23:15).

Yet despite the effort, Jewish evangelism never took off the
way Christian evangelism did. It was through Jesus that the Old
Testament prophecy of the conversion of the Gentiles to the God
of the Jews was fulfilled (as some Jewish scholars today, such as
the orthodox Jewish rabbi Pinchas Lapide, admit).

One reason that Jewish evangelism never took off the way

Christian evangelism did had to do with the kind of boasting in God the two groups were doing. Jews were boasting of having a relationship with God through the Torah, making one's adherence to the Mosaic Law the condition for conversion to God. Christians were boasting of having a relationship with God through Christ, making adherence to Christ the condition for conversion to God. Needless to say, professing faith in Christ and being baptized was a much easier way for Gentiles to come to God than being circumcised and submitting to all the regulations of the Torah (written and oral) that governed Jewish life after conversion.

A large group of people in the first century known as "Godfearers," though intellectually convinced of the folly of paganism and the truth of the Jewish religion, could not bring themselves to convert by accepting circumcision and the regulations of the Torah. Thus the very thing that many Jews held out as the basis for uniting with God became the barrier to effective evangelism. So when Christians began proclaiming the sufficiency of Christ as the basis for union with God, they made numerous converts, and in just over three hundred years the Roman Empire, archenemy of Jews and Christians alike, formally embraced the worship of Yahweh and rejected the worship of other gods.

While this still lay in the future, Paul could (and did) go to his Jewish brethren and boast of how Christ had won many converts to God through him. Christ, not Torah, was the reality that drew people to the God of the Jews (cf. John 12:32), and, thus, the reality through whom the long-prophesied conversion of the Gentiles was happening. Paul's Jewish brothers had better get on board, he would reason, if they want to be part of God's program for the ages and not be left behind, clinging to the Torah as a way of union with God when it was never intended to be that (Rom. 4:14).

Paul's discussion of his own boasting thus provides confirmation that the boasting he talks about in Romans, whether Jewish or Christian, is not boasting about one's own righteousness, contrary to the assertions of many contemporary preachers. Every passage in which Paul discusses boasting is about boasting in the greatness of God and how every human being who will can have union with him.

## Paul and James on Faith and Works

Having come this far, we are now in a position to harmonize what is said by Paul and James on the subjects of faith and works.

One passage Fundamentalists often cite as a prooftext against the Catholic view of salvation is Ephesians 2:8–9: "For by grace you have been saved through faith; and this is not your own doing, it is the gift of God—not because of works, lest any man should boast."

Typically, those who use this verse assume that the works Paul is speaking of are good works. If that were true, it would in no way conflict with Catholic theology. Note that the passage speaks of salvation as a past event—"you *have been* saved." In Greek this is the perfect tense, which denotes a past, completed action that has continuing effects in the present. The passage thus refers back to the salvation one received at the beginning of the Christian life, the effects of which are still with one through the possession of sanctifying grace.

We know from other passages in Paul that salvation also has present and future aspects (see chapter one), so the kind of salvation Paul is discussing in Ephesians 2:8–9 is *initial* salvation. It is the kind we received when we first came to God and were justified, not the kind of salvation we are now receiving (see 1 Pet. 1:8–9, Phil. 2:12) or the kind we will one day receive (see Rom. 13:11, 1 Cor. 3:15, 5:5).

Ephesians 2:8–9 does not contradict Catholic theology, even on the assumption that the "works" Paul mentions are good works, because the Catholic Church does not teach that we receive initial justification by good works. We do not have to do good works in order to come to God and be justified. According to the Council of Trent, "we are said to be justified by grace because nothing that precedes justification, whether faith or works, merits the grace of justification. For 'if it is by grace, it is no longer by works; otherwise,' as the apostle says, 'grace is no more grace' [Rom. 11:6]" (*Decree on Justification* 8).

However, Paul probably does not mean "good works" in this passage. Normally when he says "works," he means "works of Torah"—those done out of obedience to the Law of Moses. His point is to stress that we are saved by faith in Jesus Christ and not by the Mosaic Law. Jews cannot boast in front of Gentiles of having a privileged relationship with God because of the Mosaic Law and its requirement of circumcision (see Rom. 2:6–11, 17–21, 25–29, 3:21–22, 27–30).

These same elements—works, boasting, circumcision, and the Jew-Gentile distinction—are present in Ephesians 2. Paul discusses how God has shown mercy to us in Christ and, before turning to the subject of circumcision and membership in Christ, he mentions works in connection with boasting (2:9), going on to say:

> Therefore remember that at one time you Gentiles in the flesh, called the uncircumcision by what is called the circumcision . . . remember that you were at that time separated from Christ, alienated from the commonwealth of Israel. . . . But now in Christ Jesus you who once were far off have been brought near in the blood of Christ. For he is our peace, who has made us both one, and has broken down the dividing wall of hostility, by abolishing in his flesh the Law [Torah] of commandments and ordinances, that he might create in himself one new man in place of the two . . . and might reconcile us both to God in one body. . . . So then you are no longer strangers and sojourners, but you are fellow citizens with the saints and members of the household of God [Eph. 2:11–19].

Because of the common themes in both passages, Paul is probably using *works* and *boasting* here in Ephesians 2:9 in the same senses he does in Romans—that is, of Jews boasting before Gentiles of having privilege with God because of their observing the Mosaic Law. Paul says we are saved, not in that manner, but by faith— meaning faith in Christ. So in terms of salvation, no one, neither

Jew nor Gentile, can boast of having a more privileged position with God. All people are saved on the same basis: through Christ.

After rejecting works of the Mosaic Law, the apostle turns our attention away from works of the Mosaic Law and toward the kind of works a Christian *should* be interested in—good works: "For we are his workmanship, created in Christ Jesus for good works, which God prepared beforehand, that we should walk in them" (Eph. 2:10).

The sense of what Paul is saying is that it is God himself who has raised us up, Jews and Gentiles, to sit in the heavenly places because of Christ Jesus, for we received initial salvation as a gift. We obtained it by faith in Christ—which was expressed in baptism (Rom. 6:3–11)—not by works of obedience to the Mosaic Law. All of this is a grace, so neither Jewish nor Gentile Christians can boast over the other of having a superior relationship with God.

Instead, to paraphrase Ephesians 2:6–10, we Christians are the result of God's work, for he created us anew in the body of Christ so that we might do *good* works, the kind of works we *should be* concerned about, for God intended ahead of time for us to do them.

If Protestants try to put Catholics on the defensive by using Ephesians 2:8–9, they themselves are put on the defensive when Catholics cite James 2:24. Protestants are known for their claim that we are justified "by faith alone," but the expression "faith alone" (Greek, *pisteos monon*) appears only once in the Bible—in James 2:24—where it is rejected. This is a burr under the saddle for many Protestants, for if they want to use terms the way the Bible does, they would have to give up one of their chief slogans. When Catholics point this out, many Protestants attempt damage control by attacking the faith being discussed in James 2, saying it is an inferior or bad faith. Some do this by labeling it "dead faith." They treat James' statement that "faith apart from works is dead" (v. 26; see also v. 17) as if it were a definition, saying, "If faith does not produce works it is 'dead faith'; James says 'dead faith' won't save us."

But reading the context shows that James is *not* using the phrase in this way. He is not defining the term *dead faith*, a term that does not even appear in the text. He is stating a fact, not offering a definition. The invalidity of the interpretation is abundantly demonstrated when we test it by substituting "dead faith" wherever the text mentions faith. On that reading, people would be *boasting* of having dead faith (v. 14; the entire text of James 2:14–26 appears at the end of this chapter). James would be making the redundant statement that dead faith apart from works is dead (vv. 17, 26) and offering to prove that dead faith is barren (v. 20). He would be offering to show people his dead faith by his works (v. 18) and commending people ("you do well") for having dead faith (v. 19). Finally, he would be telling us that Abraham's dead faith was active with his works (v. 22) and that Abraham believed God with dead faith and it was reckoned to him as righteousness (v. 23).

Another attempt to impugn the faith in this passage uses the statement, "Even the demons believe—and shudder" (v. 19). People ask, "What kind of faith do demons have? *Mere intellectual assent.* They intellectually assent to the truths of theology, but this is as far as their faith goes."

This understanding of the faith in James 2 is closer to the truth, but it still creates problems—in fact, many of the same problems. People would be boasting of having mere intellectual assent (v. 14). James would be offering to show others his mere intellectual assent by his works (v. 18). He would be commending people for having mere intellectual assent (v. 19) and saying that Abraham's mere intellectual assent was active along with his works (v. 22), in which case it wouldn't be *mere* any more. Finally, he would be saying that Abraham's mere intellectual assent was reckoned to him as righteousness, contradicting verse 23, which tells us that mere intellectual assent is barren.

The "mere intellectual assent" solution fails just as the "dead faith" solution did. *Any* solution that impugns the faith James is talking about and calls it bad or inferior faith will fail. This can be seen by going through the passage and substituting "bad faith" and "inferior faith" wherever faith is mentioned (the reader can do that for himself). Such solutions fail because James *does not see anything wrong* with the faith he is talking about. The *faith* isn't the problem; it's being *alone* is the problem.

To understand what kind of faith James has in mind, one must avoid the temptation to read something bad into it. This is where the "mere intellectual assent" solution errs. Its advocates correctly identify verse 19 as the key to understanding the faith being discussed, which *is* intellectual assent. The problems are created by adding the pejorative term *mere*.

Leave off the *mere*, and the problems vanish. Someone can go around boasting that he intellectually assents to God's truth (v. 14), prompting James' need to show that intellectual assent without works is dead and barren (vv. 17, 20, 26). James could offer to show his intellectual assent by his works (v. 18). And he could commend a person for having intellectual assent (v. 19), while saying that even though the demons have it they still shudder at the prospect of God's wrath (v. 19). Finally, he can speak of how Abraham's intellectual assent was active with and completed by his works (v. 22), concluding that man is not justified by intellectual assent alone (v. 24).

James views intellectual assent as a good thing ("you do well," v. 19), but not as a thing that will save us by itself (vv. 14, 17, 20, 24, 26). James does not contradict Paul, because the works that must be added to intellectual assent are not works of Torah (if he said that, he *would* contradict Paul).

He also does not contradict Paul because he is talking about a different kind of justification than Paul typically does. James is discussing ongoing justification, or growth in righteousness, as illustrated by his citing the example of Abraham being justified when he offered Isaac on the altar (2:21). That was *years* after he had been initially justified and, since Abraham was not repenting of a sin at the time, we know that it is a progressive, ongoing justification that is being discussed—what some call sanctification—and sanctification does indeed involve the performance of good works and not intellectual assent alone.

It should also be noted that the *only time* the Council of Trent's

*Decree on Justification* (DJ) quotes James' statement that "a man is justified by works and not by faith alone" (2:24) is in reference to ongoing growth in righteousness (DJ, ch. 10, "The Increase of the Justification Received"). It does not apply it to initial justification because, Catholic theology holds, it is impossible for man to do anything meritorious prior to justification (DJ 8). This leads us to our next subject, which is the contemporary Catholic-Protestant dialogue on justification.

14 What does it profit, my brethren, if a man says he has faith but has not works? Can his faith save him?
15 If a brother or sister is ill-clad and in lack of daily food,
16 and one of you says to them, "Go in peace, be warmed and filled," without giving them the things needed for the body, what does it profit?
17 So faith by itself, if it has no works, is dead.

18 But some one will say, "You have faith and I have works." Show me your faith apart from your works, and I by my works will show you my faith.
19 You believe that God is one; you do well. Even the demons believe—and shudder.
20 Do you want to be shown, you shallow man, that faith apart from works is barren?
21 Was not Abraham our father justified by works, when he offered his son Isaac upon the altar?
22 You see that faith was active along with his works, and faith was completed by works,
23 and the Scripture was fulfilled which says, "Abraham believed God, and it was reckoned to him as righteousness"; and he was called the friend of God.
24 You see that a man is justified by works and not by faith alone.
25 And in the same way was not also Rahab the harlot justified by works when she received the messengers and sent them out another way?
26 For as the body apart from the spirit is dead, so faith apart from works is dead.

# 9

# Justification and Ecumenism

On October 31, 1999, the Catholic Church and the Lutheran World Federation (LWF) signed a historic document known as the *Joint Declaration on the Doctrine of Justification* (JD). This document, the fruit of almost thirty years of ecumenical dialogue, was widely misinterpreted and misrepresented by many in both the secular and the religious press. The present chapter is intended to help readers understand the most important things that the document does *and does not* say, so that they may better sift through the distortion and error that may occur in discussions of the document.

## How We Got Where We Are

The Reformation was a time of great tension between Protestants and Catholics, and for many years afterward individuals on one side frequently portrayed the other side in the least favorable light. Too often, they were interested neither in giving the other side a sympathetic hearing nor in "getting inside the heads" of the other group to understand what their writings meant. To the extent they read the works of the other party at all, they read only to look for ammunition that could be used in theological controversy.

Today, while there are still knee-jerk anti-Catholics and knee-jerk anti-Protestants, theologians and scholars on each side show a growing willingness to give a more neutral and nuanced reading to the theology of the other group. The resulting openness has borne fruit—both good and bad—in the current ecumenical movement. Among the good fruit is the progress that has been made with Lutherans on the subject of justification. Among Protestant groups, the Lutheran view of justification has always been closer to the Catholic view. (For example, Luther taught the necessity of baptism for justification, the practice of infant baptism, and the possibility of losing one's salvation.)

As scholars from the two communities read each other's writings, it became clear that the two sides were not nearly as far apart on justification as had been imagined. A number of apparent disagreements could be cleared up simply by translating Lutheran language into Catholic language and vice versa. Also, some disputes turned out to be due to differences of emphasis rather than contradictory beliefs.

Since 1972, many Catholic-Lutheran ecumenical statements on justification have been written and released by local ecumenical groups, and the extent of agreement was such that the Holy See and the Lutheran World Federation decided to explore the possibility of issuing a joint declaration on the subject. Beginning in 1994, representatives appointed by the Holy See and the Lutheran World Federation drafted and circulated a proposed text for such a joint declaration. The text was finalized in 1997, and the Lutheran World Federation approved it unanimously on June 16, 1998.

Then a hiccup occurred in the process. The Holy See announced that it would be releasing a document titled *The Response of the Catholic Church to the Joint Declaration of the Catholic Church and the Lutheran World Federation on the Doctrine of Justification* (Response). When the document was released a few days later, on June 25, the Holy See did not endorse the Joint Declaration as it stood, but expressed a number of reservations and indicated that certain points needed to be clarified. This was extremely embarrassing. The drafting of the Joint Declaration had been a years-long process, and the text had already been finalized. The concerns that were announced on June 25 should have been brought up and corresponding clarifications given *before* the text was finalized and the Lutherans went out on a limb by voting on it.

Needless to say, the Lutherans were stunned by the Holy See's sudden reticence and felt as if they had egg on their faces. Nevertheless, they summoned the tact to press ahead and discuss the clarifications the Holy See requested. The result was the drafting of an *Annex to the Joint Declaration* (Annex), which the two parties released the following year on June 11, together with the announcement that the formal signing of the Joint Declaration would take place October 31, 1999 in Augsburg, Germany.

Despite the embarrassing nature of the incident leading to the Annex, it powerfully demonstrates that the Joint Declaration is not the product of false ecumenism. That the Holy See was willing to pursue a course of action so painful to both sides, at the last minute, and not proceeding until clarifications were made, shows that the Holy See was determined that the document not misrepresent Catholic teaching.

## Important Cautions

The text of the Joint Declaration contains a number of important cautions to prevent the meaning and significance of the document from being misunderstood. These were totally disregarded by many reporters in their coverage of the document, so the reader should be informed of them up front:

1) *Neither Side Retracted Its Position, Went Back on Its History, or "Caved In"*: "[T]his Joint Declaration rests on the conviction that . . . the churches neither take the condemnations [of the sixteenth century] lightly nor do they disavow their own past" (JD 7).

2) *The Document Does Not Cover* All *of the Doctrine of Justification*: "The present Joint Declaration . . . does not cover all that either church teaches about justification; it does encompass a consensus on basic truths of the doctrine of justification and shows that the remaining differences in its explication are no longer the occasion for doctrinal condemnations" (JD 5).

3) *The Condemnations of the Reformation Era Were Not Wrong*: "Nothing is . . . taken away from the seriousness of the condem-

nations related to the doctrine of justification. . . . They remain for us 'salutary warnings' to which we must attend in our teaching and practice" (JD 42).

4) *The Document Does Not Cover All Disagreements between Catholics and Lutherans*: "[T]here are still questions of varying importance which need further clarification. These include, among other topics, the relationship between the Word of God and church doctrine, as well as ecclesiology, authority in the church, ministry, the sacraments, and the relation between justification and social ethics" (JD 43).

5) *Due to the Remaining Differences, the Two Sides Still Cannot Unite*: "Doctrinal condemnations were put forward both in the Lutheran Confessions and by the Roman Catholic Church's Council of Trent. These condemnations are still valid today and thus have a church-dividing effect" (JD 1).

One final caution:

6) *This Declaration Applies Only to Catholics and Lutherans*: This is so obvious that the document does not point it out explicitly. It is, however, important to understand that the Holy See is not saying that any and all Protestant views on justification share the same status as the ones described in the Joint Declaration. They don't. The Lutherans are the closest on justification in many respects, but many aren't nearly as close.

## The Big Picture

The Joint Declaration expresses its general conclusion a number of times, but perhaps most clearly in the following statement:

> The understanding of the doctrine of justification set forth in this Declaration shows that a consensus in basic truths of the doctrine of justification exists between Lutherans and Catholics. In light of this consensus the remaining differences of language, theological elaboration, and emphasis in the understanding of justification described in paras. 18 to 39 are acceptable. Therefore the Lutheran and the Catholic explications of justification are in their difference

open to one another and do not destroy the consensus regarding basic truths [40].

It is important to note that, though the Joint Declaration above speaks of a consensus on the basic truths regarding justification, there remain "differences of language, theological elaboration, and emphasis." In other words, the parties at times use different language, have different ways of elaborating the basic truths both agree upon, or emphasize different true concepts.

The differences do not amount to a contradiction of any of the basic truths. This is what the text means when it says that the two parties' "explications of justification are in their difference open to one another." That's a fancy way of saying that, though there may be differences of language, elaboration, and emphasis, they don't fundamentally contradict each other and so "destroy the consensus regarding basic truths."

"Thus," says the document, "the doctrinal condemnations of the sixteenth century, insofar as they relate to the doctrine of justification, appear in a new light: The teaching of the Lutheran churches presented in this Declaration does not fall under the condemnations from the Council of Trent. The condemnations in the Lutheran Confessions do not apply to the teaching of the Roman Catholic Church presented in this Declaration" (JD 41).

Note that the above passage states that the condemnations of the Council of Trent do not apply to "the teaching of the Lutheran churches *presented in this Declaration*." Teachings of the Lutheran churches not presented in the Joint Declaration can and do fall under Trent's condemnations.

Certain ideas of other Protestant groups on justification *are* rejected by Trent. The idea that there was a single Protestant view of justification would have been just as much a myth in the 1500s as it is today. The Council of Trent was faced with a bewildering array of mutually contradictory Protestant ideas on justification. What the Council did was to condemn the gravest errors, regardless of which individuals or groups were advocating them. As a result, the condemnations issued by Trent did not, as a body, apply to any one Protestant or school of Protestantism.

Thus Trent never intended some of its condemnations to apply to Lutherans. The dialogue that has taken place since Trent has revealed that additional condemnations—of doctrinal errors regarding justification—also do not apply to the teachings of Lutherans, or at least the Lutherans signing the Joint Declaration.

One of the dialogues that laid the groundwork for the Joint Declaration was a 1986 study done by representatives of the German conference of bishops and the parallel German Lutheran body. Joseph Cardinal Ratzinger served as the Catholic chairman of the Joint Ecumenical Commission responsible for the document, which was published in English as *The Condemnations of the Reformation Era: Do They Still Divide?*[11] This study concluded that the condemnations found in canons 2, 4–13, 16, 24, and 32 of Trent's *Decree on Justification* (DJ) did not apply to modern German Lutherans. This list was not exhaustive, however, since other canons in Trent's Decree were never thought to apply to Lutherans. Canon 1, for example, condemns those who say we can be justified by our own works, while canon 3 condemns those who would say we do not need the grace of the Holy Spirit to be justified—both of which ideas were as firmly condemned by Lutherans as by Catholics.

## Seven Topics

One of the most important sections in the Joint Declaration, "Explicating the Common Understanding of Justification," clarifies seven contentious issues: (1) Human Powerlessness and Sin in Relation to Justification, (2) Justification as Forgiveness of Sins and Making Righteous, (3) Justification by Faith and through Grace,

---

[11] *The Condemnations of the Reformation Era: Do They Still Divide?*, Karl Lehmann and Wolfhart Pannenberg, eds., (Minneapolis: Fortress Press, 1990).

(4) The Justified as Sinner, (5) Law and Gospel, (6) Assurance of Salvation, and (7) The Good Works of the Justified. We will look at each of these.

## 1. HUMAN POWERLESSNESS AND SIN IN RELATION TO JUSTIFICATION

Lutherans have often used language suggesting not only that humans are powerless to seek justification without God's grace (something with which Catholics agree) but also that humans are unable to cooperate in any way with God's grace and must receive justification in a "merely passive" manner. When Catholics do not go along with this extreme language, Lutherans have seen that as a denial of man's inability to seek justification without God's grace. The Joint Declaration rectifies this misunderstanding:

> We confess together that all persons depend completely on the saving grace of God for their salvation . . . for as sinners they stand under God's judgment and are incapable of turning by themselves to God to seek deliverance, of meriting their justification before God, or of attaining salvation by their own abilities. Justification takes place solely by God's grace. . . . When Catholics say that persons "cooperate" in preparing for and accepting justification . . . they see such personal consent as itself an effect of grace, not as an action arising from innate human abilities [19–20].

Unfortunately, this section of the Joint Declaration went on to use the Lutheran description of man as "merely passive" with respect to justification (n. 21) without fully explaining it. The Response of the Holy See stressed that this be clarified further. Consequently, the *Annex to the Joint Declaration* made the following affirmation:

> The working of God's grace does not exclude human action: God effects everything, the willing and the achievement, therefore we are called to strive (cf. Phil. 2:12ff.). "As soon as the Holy Spirit has initiated his work of regeneration and renewal in us through the Word and the holy sacraments, it is certain that we can and

must cooperate by the power of the Holy Spirit . . ." [*The Formula of Concord*, FC SD II, 64f. (Annex 2C)].

## 2. JUSTIFICATION AS FORGIVENESS OF SINS AND MAKING RIGHTEOUS

A perennial subject of disagreement has been the nature of justification. Frequently, Lutherans have characterized it as only a forgiveness of sins, whereas the Church insists that it is more than this. The Joint Declaration makes this statement:

> We confess together that God forgives sin by grace and at the same time frees human beings from sin's enslaving power and imparts the gift of new life in Christ. When persons come by faith to share in Christ, God no longer imputes to them their sin and through the Holy Spirit effects in them an active love. These two aspects of God's gracious action are not to be separated.
>
> When Lutherans emphasize that the righteousness of Christ is our righteousness, their intention is above all to insist that the sinner is granted righteousness before God in Christ through the declaration of forgiveness and that only in union with Christ is one's life renewed. When they stress that God's grace is forgiving love ("the favor of God"), they do not thereby deny the renewal of the Christian's life [22–23].

This description of justification as both forgiveness of sins and inward renewal reflects Trent's statement that justification "is not only a remission of sins but also the sanctification and renewal of the inward man" (DJ 7).

Some Catholics have been concerned that this section of the Joint Declaration does not explicitly mention what Trent called the "formal cause" of justification, which refers to the *kind* of righteousness one receives in justification. According to Trent (DJ 7, can. 11), there is a single formal cause of justification: sanctifying grace (see L. Ott, *Fundamentals of Catholic Dogma*, 251–252). The nature of sanctifying grace has not been finally determined. According to the common view, that of the Thomists, sanctifying grace is a quality that God gives the soul and that always accompanies but is nevertheless distinct from the virtue of charity. According to the less common view, that of the Scotists, sanctifying grace and charity are the same thing.

The Joint Declaration does not raise this discussion, perhaps on the grounds that it involves what is still an open question among Catholics, perhaps also from unwillingness to delve into scholastic terminology not used by the partner in ecumenical dialogue. The document is simply content to say that in justification God no longer imputes sin (that is, he forgives or remits it) and that he creates charity in the believer. The omission of the term *sanctifying grace* in favor of the term *charity* is not to be construed as an endorsement of the Scotist view. That would misread a document that is not intended to settle questions that are still open for Catholics; much less is it intended to endorse the less common of two views.

### 3. Justification by Faith and through Grace

Two key Protestant slogans are "justification by grace alone" and "justification by faith alone." (These do not contradict each other since they are speaking on different levels of what causes justification.) Catholics have never had trouble affirming the first slogan, though Protestants commonly believe they do. Both Catholics and Lutherans often have thought that Catholics must condemn all possible uses of the second slogan, but this is not the case.

The confusion is based in a misreading of Canon 9 of Trent's *Decree on Justification*, which states that "if anyone says that the sinner is justified by faith alone, so that thus he understands[12] nothing else is required to cooperate in order to obtain the grace of justification, and that it is not in any way necessary that he be

---

[12] In Latin the phrase corresponding to "so that thus he understands" is *ita ut intelligat*. The term *intelligat* can also be translated as "perceives" or "feels." This construction in Latin serves to explain which understanding of the term "faith alone" is being condemned.

prepared and disposed by the action of his own will, let him be anathema."[13]

As a careful reading of this canon shows, not every use of the "faith alone" formula is rejected, but only those that are understood to mean that "nothing else is required." If it is acknowledged that things besides the theological virtue of faith are required, then use of the "faith alone" formula does not fall under the condemnation. The Council therefore condemned one meaning of the formula, not all possible uses. The classic Catholic alternative to saying that we are saved "by faith alone" is to say, "We are saved by faith, hope, and charity." It is possible, however, for these two formulas to be equivalent in meaning.

Charity—the supernatural love of God—is what ultimately unites the soul to God. It therefore is recognized as the "form" of the virtues, that which binds them together and gives them their fullest expression. Catholic theologians have historically talked about virtues being "formed" or "unformed," based on whether they are united with charity. If a person has both faith and charity, for example, he is said to have "formed faith by charity" (*fides formata caritate*); if he has faith without charity, he has "unformed faith" (*fides informis*).

St. Paul tells us that anyone who has charity also has faith and hope, for charity "believes all things, hopes all things" (1 Cor. 13:7). Thus if one has formed faith, one has not only faith and charity, but also hope.

This is why the two formulas—"faith alone" and "faith, hope, and charity"—can be equivalent. To talk about formed faith is

---

[13] In conciliar documents, such as those of Trent, the term *anathema* does not mean damned by God. It referred to a canon law penalty whereby the pope used a particular ceremony to excommunicate someone. Such excommunications were not automatic, and only comparatively rarely in history was this kind of excommunication applied. The penalty no longer exists, having lapsed with the promulgation of the 1983 *Code of Canon Law*. However, the doctrinal value of canons using this term remains (that is, any doctrinal claim rejected in such canons is still infallibly rejected).

to talk about a faith that is accompanied by hope and charity. Consequently, if one asserts that we are justified by faith alone—meaning by formed faith—then the phrase is not being used in a way that falls under Trent's condemnation.

Different Protestants mean different things by the "faith alone" slogan. A few really do mean that one is justified by intellectual belief alone, without hope or charity. Others, many American Evangelicals among them, appear to believe one is justified by faith plus hope, which is trust in God for salvation. Many others (including the Lutherans who signed the Joint Declaration) believe that charity, the principle behind good works, always accompanies justifying faith. So they believe in justification by formed faith.

This is the sense reflected in the Joint Declaration, which states that "justifying faith . . . includes hope in God and love for him. Such a faith is active in love and thus the Christian cannot and should not remain without works" (JD 25). This understanding lies behind such statements in the Joint Declaration as "We confess together that persons are justified by faith in the gospel 'apart from works prescribed by the law' (Rom. 3:28)" (JD 31). The understanding of justifying faith as formed faith also lies behind the statement of the Annex: "Justification takes place 'by grace alone' (JD 15 and 16), by faith alone; the person is justified 'apart from works' (Rom. 3:28, cf. JD 25)" (Annex 2C).

The equivalence of the two formulas has been noted for many years in Catholic circles. For example, the 1985 German Conference of Bishops' adult catechism states:

> Catholic doctrine . . . says that only a faith alive in graciously bestowed love can justify. Having "mere" faith without love, merely considering something true, does not justify us. But if one understands faith in the full and comprehensive biblical sense, then faith includes conversion, hope, and love—and the Lutheran ["faith alone"] formula can have a *good Catholic sense.*[14]

---

[14] *The Church's Confession of Faith: A Catholic Catechism for Adults*, (San Francisco: Ignatius Press, 1987), 200; emphasis in original.

Similarly, the 1986 ecumenical study of which Cardinal Ratzinger was a part drew this conclusion: "If we translate from one language to another, then . . . Protestant doctrine understands substantially under the one word 'faith' what Catholic doctrine (following 1 Cor. 13:13) sums up in the triad of 'faith, hope, and love.' But in this case the mutual rejections in this question can be viewed as no longer applicable today" (Lehmann and Pannenberg, op. cit.).

It should be explicitly pointed out, though, that the signing of the Joint Declaration definitely does not mean that Catholics should begin using an unbiblical formula to describe the way in which we are justified.

The phrase, *pisteos monon* ("faith alone"), appears only once in the New Testament, in James 2:24, where it is rejected. For this reason alone, anyone who wants to imitate the language of the Bible should not use this formula.

Further, the formula is intrinsically confusing. In common parlance, the term *faith* is a synonym for *belief*. When coupled with the word *alone* and used to describe the method of our justification, it communicates to most people the erroneous idea that we can be saved by intellectual belief alone. This has been a danger since the apostolic age. Some in the first century didn't read Paul's language carefully enough when he said in Romans 3:28 that we are justified by faith and not by works of the Law. They misunderstood him to be saying that we are saved by faith alone (rather than by faith in Christ apart from the Law of Moses), and it was the misunderstanding of Paul that James was condemning in his epistle. That's the reason James goes into the subject.

It's also a problem for modern Protestants. The phrase "faith alone" is so confusing that Evangelicals themselves constantly have to explain what the formula does *not* mean—that we are saved by belief apart from trust or that we will be saved even if we do not truly repent of our sins.

All around, the phrase "faith alone" is a bad idea, and the Joint Declaration in no way encourages Catholics to use it as part of their theological vocabulary. What the Joint Declaration does is strike a delicate balance on the subject of the formula. It acknowledges—rightly—that the formula is being used by the Lutheran World Federation in a sense that does not fall under the condemnations of Trent because the LWF has defined the term *faith* broadly enough that it equals "faith, hope, and charity" in the Catholic sense. The Joint Declaration thus acknowledges that the LWF is using the phrase in a way that does not fall under Trent's condemnations, but it does not in any way encourage Catholics to begin using this highly problematic formula.

This is why the formula never appears in any of the "we confess together" passages of the Joint Declaration. If it did appear in one of those, the document would have encouraged Catholics to use the formula in their own theological vocabulary. Rightly, it does not do so. It acknowledges that the Lutherans' use of the formula among themselves is not condemned by Trent, but that doesn't mean we Catholics should start using it among ourselves. It would bring on terrible confusion if they did so.

### 4. THE JUSTIFIED AS SINNER

The section of the Joint Declaration that most concerned the Holy See was not, as some may think, the part dealing with justification by grace and faith. Indeed, the Holy See did not ask for any clarifications on that subject. Instead, the most difficult section was the one dealing with the classic Lutheran expression that man is "at once righteous and a sinner" (Latin: *simul iustus et peccator*).

The Holy See was concerned to uphold the Catholic teaching that "in baptism everything that is really sin is taken away, and so, in those who are born anew there is nothing that is hateful to God. It follows that the concupiscence that remains in the baptized is not, properly speaking, sin" (Response, Clarification 1).

This controversy goes back to a major dispute at the time of the Protestant breakaway, when Lutherans wished to say that the concupiscence (disordered desire) that remains in the individual after justification still has the character of sin. The Catholic Church taught what it always had, which is that concupiscence "has never

[been] understood to be called sin in the sense that it is truly and properly sin in those born again, but in the sense that it is from sin and inclines to sin" (Trent, *Decree on Original Sin* 5).

The *Annex to the Joint Declaration* responds by conceding that "it can be recognized from a Lutheran perspective that [concupiscent] desire can become the opening through which sin attacks" (2B). Concupiscence is a vulnerability that leads to sin, but is not itself sin.

Because concupiscence can lead to sin,

> we would be wrong were we to say that we are without sin (1 John 1:8–10, cf. JD 28). "All of us make many mistakes" (Jas. 3:2). This recalls to us the persisting danger that comes from the power of sin and its action in Christians. To this extent, Lutherans and Catholics can together understand the Christian as *simul iustus et peccator*, despite their different approaches to this subject as expressed in JD 29–30 [Annex 2A].

Christians thus remain sinners in the sense that they are inclined to sin by concupiscence, but they do not remain sinners in the sense that God's forgiveness and justification takes away from them all that is properly called sin. Annex 2A further says,

> We are truly and inwardly renewed by the action of the Holy Spirit, remaining always dependent on his work in us. "So if anyone is in Christ, there is a new creation: everything old has passed away; see, everything has become new!" (2 Cor. 5:17). The justified do not remain sinners in this sense.

## 5. Law and Gospel

Lutherans historically have drawn an overly sharp distinction between law and gospel, to the point that in Lutheran theology these can become abstract philosophical ideas. Unfortunately, this is not the way the terms are used in Scripture. When the Bible refers to "the Law," it almost always means the Torah, the Law of Moses, which not only makes legal demands but promises God's grace. Similarly, when the Bible speaks about "the gospel," it does not envision a set of unconditional promises; salvation in Christ is conditional.

A consequence of Lutheranism's rigid divide between law and gospel is that Lutherans have at times used language suggesting that Christ is given to us only as a Savior to be believed in, not also as a Lawgiver to be obeyed. To correct this, the Joint Declaration contains this affirmation: "We also confess that God's commandments retain their validity for the justified and that Christ has by his teaching and example expressed God's will, which is a standard for the conduct of the justified also" (31).

Also because of the sharp division made between law and gospel, Lutherans at times have been suspicious of Catholic discussion of Christ as Lawgiver, thinking that this may reduce Christ to being just another Moses, bringing legal demands rather than salvation. The Joint Declaration addresses this concern:

> Because the law as a way to salvation has been fulfilled and over-
> come through the gospel, Catholics can say that Christ is not a
> lawgiver in the manner of Moses. When Catholics emphasize that
> the righteous are bound to observe God's commandments, they
> do not thereby deny that through Jesus Christ God has mercifully
> promised to his children the grace of eternal life [33].

## 6. Assurance of Salvation

This is one of the most misunderstood subjects relating to justi-fication. Too often both sides have been needlessly polarized on the question of what kind of assurance one can have regarding salvation.

Too often Lutherans have made it sound as if one can have absolute assurance that one is or will be saved. But even they will admit that, because of the fallenness of the human intellect and the capacity for self-deception (not to mention the possibility of falling from grace, which Lutherans acknowledge), one cannot have infallible certitude regarding salvation.

Too often Catholics have made it sound as if it were not possible to have any assurance of salvation. This is based on a misreading of the Council of Trent. All the Council stated was that a person cannot "know with the certainty of faith, *which cannot be subject to error*" (DJ 9, emphasis added), and that he cannot know "with an absolute and *infallible* certainty, [that he will] have that great gift of perseverance even to the end, unless he shall have learned this by a special revelation" (DJ 16, emphasis added).

The two sides are thus in agreement: assurance is possible, but not infallible assurance (barring special revelation). Thus the Joint Declaration affirms:

> We confess together that the faithful can rely on the mercy and promises of God. In spite of their own weakness and the manifold threats to their faith, on the strength of Christ's death and resurrection they can build on the effective promise of God's grace in Word and Sacrament and so be sure of this grace. . . . In trust in God's promise [believers] are assured of their salvation, but are never secure looking at themselves. . . . No one may doubt God's mercy and Christ's merit. Every person, however, may be concerned about his salvation when he looks upon his own weaknesses and shortcomings [34–36].

## 7. THE GOOD WORKS OF THE JUSTIFIED

Lutherans have been suspicious that the Church holds that one must do good works in order to enter a state of justification. This has never been the case. In Catholic teaching, one is not capable of doing supernaturally good works outside of a state of justification because one's soul lacks the virtue of charity—the thing that makes good works good. Consequently, the Council of Trent taught that "none of those things that precede justification, whether faith or works, merit the grace of justification" (DJ 8).

The Joint Declaration thus stresses that good works are a consequence of entering a state of justification, not the cause of entering it:

> We confess together that good works—a Christian life lived in faith, hope, and love—follow justification and are its fruits. When

the justified live in Christ and act in the grace they receive, they bring forth, in biblical terms, good fruit. . . .

According to Catholic understanding, good works, made possible by grace and the working of the Holy Spirit, contribute to growth in grace, so that the righteousness that comes from God is preserved and communion with Christ is deepened. When Catholics affirm the "meritorious" character of good works, they wish to say that, according to the biblical witness, a reward in heaven is promised to these works. Their intention is to emphasize the responsibility of persons for their actions, not to contest the character of those works as gifts, or far less to deny that justification always remains the unmerited gift of grace [37–38].

## General Appraisal of the Joint Declaration

The Joint Declaration provides a valuable service in clearing away a significant number of misunderstandings regarding justification, but at times the language it uses is confusing. The Holy See acknowledged this when it issued the *Response to the Joint Declaration*, insisting on a number of further clarifications before the Joint Declaration could be signed.

Further, the Joint Declaration gives very little attention to, or simply omits, some aspects of the doctrine of justification. I very much would have liked to see the Joint Declaration further explain the sense in which Scripture describes eternal life as a reward for "perseverance in working good" (Rom. 2:6–7). More attention could have been devoted to the subject of progressive justification, by which we grow in righteousness over the course of the Christian life. And we could have done with a fuller treatment of the way justification is lost through sin and then regained.

One of the most conspicuous absences from the Joint Declaration is a discussion of the language James uses in chapter 2 of his epistle. James is cited only once, a reference to 3:2, which simply acknowledges that "we all stumble in many things." While we're at the business of reconciliation, it would have been good to have a discussion of the way in which James and Paul are to be reconciled, especially when James directly intends to clarify misunderstandings of Paul. Despite these limitations, the Joint Declaration is significant for ecumenical dialogue and worthy of close study.

## Consequences for Apologetics

The Joint Declaration also has significance for apologists. It is a watershed in the history of Catholic apologetics as related to Protestantism.

For apologists, the Joint Declaration calls for a change in tone regarding justification. It will be increasingly difficult for apologists to maintain a confrontational stance on this topic when the Church is taking a conciliatory stance. Concretely, it will be difficult for confrontational approaches to be taken on the seven topics from section 4 of the Joint Declaration. Those who insist on such approaches increasingly will find themselves facing the rejoinder, "How can you say that when your own Church says something different?"

Consequently, it is better for the apologist to take a conciliatory approach to justification. This will have a number of positive effects. It will keep our language in conformity with the language of the Church. It will force us to learn the Church's theology of justification in greater depth rather than simply repeat stock formulas. And it will make our message more appealing to Protestants who are interested in becoming Catholic.

# Glossary

The terms that apply to the study of salvation are many and often unfamiliar. This glossary is therefore included. The reader should be reminded that while each word does convey a slightly different notion, the terms are used by the writers of the Bible in an overlapping, often interchangeable manner.

The reader should also be aware that each definition given below is meant to convey the basic, root idea of a term rather than the complete theology associated with it. For example, *justify* is defined as "to make right (just) with God." This conveys the root idea but does not examine whether justification occurs only at the beginning of the believer's life, whether it can be lost, how it is received, or whether it involves one's receiving legal or actual righteousness or both. For that kind of information, read the chapters of this book.

*Atone*: To reconcile by making amends or compensation (noun: *atonement*).

*Attrition*: Sorrow for our sins based on any supernatural motive other than charity.

*Charity*: The theological virtue whereby we love God above all things for his own sake and whereby we love our neighbor as ourselves for God's sake.

*Contrition*: Sorrow for our sins, which is divided into perfect contrition and imperfect contrition (attrition).

*Expiate*: To make amends or provide compensation (noun: *expiation*).

*Faith*: The theological virtue whereby we believe all that God reveals because it is revealed by God.

*Formed faith*: The theological virtue of faith made active by the virtue of charity.

*Hope*: The theological virtue whereby we trust God for all the grace that is needed for our salvation.

*Justify*: To make right (just) with God (noun: *justification*).

*Merit*: (1) Something which is given as a reward, (2) something for which a reward is given.

*Perfect contrition*: Sorrow for our sins that is based on charity, including repentance and the will to do what is needed to be reconciled with God.

*Redeem*: To buy back (e.g., from slavery to sin, from death, from danger of going to hell) (noun: *redemption*).

*Repent*: (1) To turn from a particular sin and firmly resolve not to do it in the future, (2) to turn from sins generally, firmly resolving to live according to God's law in accord with the conditions of this life.

*Righteousness*: The quality of a person who has been justified, or made right with God. Righteousness may be actual (ontological), legal, or behavioral.

*Sanctify*: To make holy (noun: *sanctification*).

*Satisfy*: To reconcile by providing adequate compensation (noun: *satisfaction*).

*Save*: To rescue, whether from temporal dangers (such as the danger of dying in battle) or eternal dangers (such as the danger of going to hell). In Greek and Latin, often carries the idea of health or a restoration to health (noun: *salvation*).

*Soteriology*: The branch of theology concerned with the doctrine of salvation.

# Scripture Index

## *Old Testament*

## New Testament

# Subject Index